The 'Thrival' Guide To Work and Life

HOW TO WIN IN BOTH!

by

Rubi Ho

Orphan, 'Street Punk Monk,'
Fortune 500 Enterprise Executive Coach and Organizational Optimizer,
MA, MS, Executive MBA

ISBN: 978-1-71695-276-0 (sc)
ISBN: 978-1-71695-633-1 (hc)
ISBN: 978-1-71695-275-3 (e)

Library of Congress Control Number: 2020906958

Lulu Publishing Services rev. date: 04/24/2020

Dedications and Gratitude

This book is dedicated to those individuals who simply want to be "better than they were yesterday." Be courageous, be bold, and never, ever, ever give up.

I want to thank all of the people both professionally and personally who I have been blessed to cross paths with over my lifetime. There are too many names to mention, but you know who you are. There is no way I could be who I am without your presence in my life.

I want to thank all of my "pre-readers," who dedicated their time, passion, and discipline to helping make my book the very best it could be. I am humbled by your willingness to contribute and so blessed for the life-long friendships I have with you all. I am indebted to you all for your efforts and commitment.

I want to thank my beautiful wife, my precious son, and saintly Ya-Ya, who takes care of our homestead while I am away and on the road hours upon hours and days upon days. I love you all from here to infinity.

I want to thank my brothers and sisters, who have been connected with me throughout the years, through thick and thin, and through the sharing of our joys and sorrows. I love you all very much!

Last but not least, I dedicate this book to God, to Infinite Source, and to the Holy Spirit. May this book land in the hands of someone who might need a little nudge, desire to become their highest self, or who is simply pursuing peace and joy in all that they do.

Amen.

Foreword

What I personally wrote to Rubi Ho after having read his book not once, but 3 times. I hope you do the same! It's that powerful of a read!

'Rubi,

I have finished your book for the 3rd read. I read in logical order, and I read in reverse order (last chapter 1st), and I read from page 71-142, then page 1-71. (Don't ask but I learned this technique long ago. ☺)

After much thought on this work of yours I have to say that it's " painfully insightful". Most writers try to be in self-help category, and most fail. Your work has a presence that is stated in a picture I have in my library, and have had since I was in college. This picture always " grounds me", and gives me the insight to be committed to the path I am about to take. But it also makes me very aware when the path I took has run its course . People think there is a major point in their lives of the "the road not taken" by Robert Frost. But I have learned years ago life is many of these crossroads.

All this di-tribe to be said that I can offer you one thing about this work you have toiled over. My review is as follows:

"Painful Past, Grounded Reality, Committed Mentoring"

You pull back the terribly painful curtain of your beginnings, You devise a series of CORE Life Values, and once you succeed, you begin with mentoring. This work isn't self-help, it very acutely says, you are not alone, and you have never been alone. Just ask for help, and if no one is there to assist, here is a plan that worked for me.

I love you brother, and I will never forget what you have done for me.

GT'

Table of Contents

About The Book

Life is complicated. So is work. Don't be so hard on yourself.

The truth is we never really "get there." Simply strive for perfect intent. Intend to thrive. You'll mess up a lot. So what? Keep pressing forward.

Your joy and peace depend on it. The people you work with and live with depend on it. The bottom line is this: You will *never* regret living a life that is focused on 'thrival' versus survival.

There is no perfect path to thriving. This book is simply *my* way in helping others, including myself, accomplish peace and joy. I hope it benefits you as well.

I don't have all the answers. I simply know what has worked for me and countless other individuals and leaders who I've personally been blessed to help.

Here's to creating *your* thriving life!

Rubi

Introduction

It's time to take charge! There's *surviving* and then there's *thriving.*

Which would you rather do: survive or thrive? Simply surviving, in my opinion, is not enough. "Survival mode" can even create complacency in life and work.

Surviving *is* important when we are cornered and barely scraping by to stay alive. Our motivation to stay alive is very high and our efforts are very intentional. But once basic survival is secured, *just* surviving is not enough.

My intention is for you to *thrive.* It's about doing *more* than enough. It's about going the extra mile, giving your very best. It's about achieving your highest, most fulfilled self, *both* in life *and* at work.

Instead of providing you with a "survival guide" then, I'm giving you a "Thrival Guide."

This book is about optimizing your career and the performance of your team and your organization. It's *also* about living a rich and fulfilled personal life. It's about winning in both areas. It's about thriving!

Ask yourself two questions:

- Do you know where you'd like to be going or what you'd like to be doing - but see no way to get there from here?
- Do you feel like your opponent or environment has you outmatched and you just can't get past him or it?

It's time to wake-up from your numb life, whip yourself into shape, seize the reins, and lead that horse you're riding where you want it to go! I've done it, so I am proof that it can be done.

When I came to America, I had nothing but what I was wearing.

Since then, I have become an enterprise executive coach and organizational consultant to Fortune 500 companies and their leaders.

I've worked with more than eighty companies in various industries and helped them to achieve their goals by optimizing their leaders, teams and the way they do things.

The truth is, the same skills that make us great in life also make us great in business. So let's learn these skills now.

The end goal, whether personal or corporate, is the same: happiness and peace.

I simply desire ONE thing for you: to be happy and at peace.

We'll explore how being unquestionably in charge of your life leads to greater peace of mind - and some practical exercises to put you back in charge - in the chapters to come.

Chapter 1

Thrive At Work

I have only one intent in writing this book: to share as much as possible of what I have learned so far in my lifetime of being obsessed with thriving, happiness and peace.

My goal is to help you get there too. Regardless of how high you plan to climb on the corporate ladder or how large or small the company you work for is, the same set of principles apply. I am intimately familiar with these principles. Please bear with me for a moment as I prove this to you.

Once you've seen my track record, I hope you will decide to put this book's principles into action into your own business and your own life.

I spent nearly a decade at a Fortune 100 consumer products and research company before creating my own executive coaching and *optimization* firm. Now, I spend my time helping countless organizations of all shapes and sizes to optimize their leaders, teams, corporate performance, achievements, and overall peace and happiness.

I didn't start out with a family endowment or highly educated parents. In fact, my family came to the United States as penniless refugees during the Vietnam War.

My siblings and I were soon orphaned by my mother's death at the hands of a drunk driver. A judge gambled on allowing us to stay in the care of my eldest sister, instead of being separated in the foster care system.

We had nothing. No advantages, except adversity. Some might

suggest that my difficult childhood is the source of my obsession with success - and they'd be right.

During my years with my Fortune 100 consumer products and research employer, I got a lot done. By using some of the methods I'll share in this book, I was able to:

- Join my Fortune 100 employer's corporate training division
- Earn my second master's degree in Organizational Management
- Complete my executive coaching certificate from Penn State, and
- Create a leadership program within my corporate department

Since then, I've drastically expanded my capacity to help *all* businesses succeed by starting my own coaching and consulting firm. I've developed my own corporate optimization system, called SAOL (Strategy, Agility, Organizational Health, and Leadership).

I've done things like:

- Served as the executive coach for a budding deputy CFO of a $4 billion company, who has since become COO of a $100 billion company.
- Worked with a $1 billion sales executive to transform his team relationships and empower his entire department.
- Optimized team performance with the site manager of a multi-billion dollar manufacturing site.
- Worked with the leadership teams of various healthcare companies to transform the vision, strategies, goals and entire culture of their businesses and nonprofit processes and models.
- Created a leadership coaching bootcamp for HR managers and consultants in a multi-billion dollar oil company.
- Solved convergence and alignment problems for the primary IT, Operations, Legal and Compliance departments of a $32 billion not for profit energy company.

- Optimized an executive's leadership and relationships with her peers and team who are responsible for over $500 million of revenue to the company's bottom line.
- Partnered with the executive team of a $25 million nonprofit to help transform the vision, strategy and milestones.
- Helped launch over two dozen new executive coaching and consulting careers via my SAOL coaching and consulting certification.
- Partnered with an executive director to help successfully converge over 40 independent engineering firms within a single association and map out their three-year key strategies.
- Clarified career path focus, company roles, and leadership roles for countless individual clients within their corporations.
- Dissolved alignment issues, communication issues, priority disagreements, direction issues, and value added issues for countless professional teams.

I tell you this, not so that you'll be impressed with me, but so that you'll be impressed with *you*. This is what is possible for an individual when the proper success principles and strategies are followed, regardless of any advantages or disadvantages.

In this book, I will do my best to teach you these principles as thoroughly as I can without the benefit of face-to-face conversation.

> One of the first principles is this: **To achieve staggering success, it's necessary to love, *be talented and have demand for* what you do.**

When you think about what's been holding you back so far, why you haven't met your business or career milestones, what comes to mind?

When you think about the idea of becoming "obsessed with success," what feels like it's holding you back?

Some of you may feel excited and enthusiastic about optimizing your success. "I can't wait," you're thinking. "Let's get to it!"

But for many of you, there may be a sense that meeting these milestones simply isn't the best use of your time and energy. For you, it is entirely possible that you are in the wrong job.

This is an important principle for both employees and managers to understand. That's because it's difficult to make an employee a top performer if they don't love what they do - and it's almost impossible to get top performance out of *yourself* if you're working in a role that's not compatible with your skills and values.

The good news is, here we'll discuss techniques to get teams on the right mission for their organization and skill sets, and help them experience the importance of their work.

We'll also explore signs that employees might actually be better off - and higher-performing - in a different role. For me, discrepancy between my role and my passion and skills was what caused me to leave my Fortune 100 employer. I was extremely successful there - but I was *not* pursuing what I loved. I was far more interested in "resolution driving," and in the optimization of people and organizations, than in routine business operations.

There came a day when I realized that, although it would be scary and difficult, I had to quit and move on. In fact, I was so sure of my direction and had such good standing with my employer that they allowed me to leave on my own terms with six months' notice. I still have very good friends there, and think fondly of that company today.

My leap into enterprise executive coaching and consulting was *very* tough for me mentally and emotionally. I was giving up certainty and success to go into an unknown, unproven territory.

I knew deep down that I had the skills and natural talent. I was looking at a major short-term pay cut (more than 50% of my six figure salary) - but with the potential for massive success further down the road. Was the trade-off worth it?

Following my instincts turned out to be correct. I soon found my "sweet spot," and now I deliver tens of millions of dollars in value to organizations of every shape and size each year. We'll learn more about how I accomplish this - and how you can learn the same skills - later.

This career transition was a difficult leap of faith, but it was one that I knew I had to make. The naysayers were all around me. In my head, I kept saying to myself: *Are you crazy? Why would you leave a place of stability and good pay?*

In my life, a number of people were saying: "Are you crazy? Why would you leave a place of stability and good pay?!"

Now I'm doing what I love, and I am very effective at it. Don't take it from *me*. Ask my clients and they will tell you how, together, we have transformed and optimized their businesses and their people.

The same transformation is possible for you, and your team.

At the beginning of my consulting career, I worked with clients for much less than I'd made at my Fortune 100 employer. I did this because I knew I needed things that money can't buy: practice and experience.

No one gets good at anything just by taking classes or gaining academic knowledge. I needed hands-on experience, and I needed good word of mouth.

Soon, I had both. So much so that I was asked to become a partner in an existing consulting firm, and have spent time as an adjunct professor of leadership coaching for several well-known universities across the country.

As I practiced teaching executives and teams to be better leaders, I saw firsthand time and time again how my clients' minds were so wrapped up in their business priorities. It became clear that focusing on *just* their leadership behavior wasn't enough of a motivator for them. Leadership is not a skill practiced in isolation, after all: it's a way of exercising business and life skills.

My clients wanted to know how to see team-wide and organization-wide results. They wanted to know how to solve the specific problem that was in front of them. Those problems could come in any shape or size, from personnel conflicts to technological crises, from supply chain blockages to profit issues. Realizing this, I began to integrate their business priorities into my coaching sessions with them.

This turned out to be *exactly* what my clients needed: a trusted confidant who could be a sounding board and guide *both* on the business side *and* while offering the leadership guidance they needed to take their companies, careers and teams to the next level.

The merging of *both* business *and* leadership skills gave rise to my consulting and coaching methodology, called SAOL (pronounced 'soul').

Slowly but surely, my clientele grew through word of mouth. The bulk of my early clients were mid-level managers. Through my success stories, I was hired by senior managers, then directors, then vice presidents, and then executives. Before I knew it, I was working with boards and with entire companies. At all of these levels, the same methodology worked!

I started by becoming intimately familiar with my clients' business strategies, their mission, their vision, their financial goals, their team goals, their succession criteria, their talent management plan, their training and development strategies, their RIF (Reduction in Force) strategies, their financial goals, their KPIs (key performance indicators), and all other critical areas impacting business performance.

None of my clients' results have *ever* been accomplished by me alone. Like any coach, I can only produce results as good as the players I'm coaching. It's the executives, directors, managers, and individuals who do the work to implement the principles that ultimately lead to success.

This is great news! It means that your level of success is based, not on the skills of your teammates, but on *your own ability* to find and implement the best principles and methodologies to reach your goals. I have been truly blessed. My apparent disadvantages early in life showed me a way of problem-solving and optimization that few people see.

Growing up as an orphaned refugee, I had to learn to work with every conceivable type of person and personality. I had to learn to solve problems even when and where no resources existed. I had to learn to make seemingly impossible situations *work*.

This gave me a perspective that simply can't be learned in *any* business school.

You see, the *primary* thing that has allowed me to help so many is *not* that I am smarter than anyone. I've simply been exposed to so many unique circumstances, and have had the opportunity to help so many individuals and businesses in so many different ways. I have even learned to teach others how to do what I do.

These skills can be taught and learned, so you don't have to go through the desperate circumstances or decades of trial and error I went through to develop this process. But remember this: anyone who wants to learn this art needs to bring their own 'street cred' and hands-on experience of life as well.

Along the way, I've failed often (like all successful people), and I've learned a tremendous amount from my failures. In my opinion, *that* is the mark of a successful work life.

No life is a perfectly smooth ride. Life is always full of ups and downs. But what we *learn* from these makes the difference between ultimate success and failing to achieve our goals.

As an outsider with a broad perspective, I have the ability to see what others can't initially see for themselves. Being able to see more clearly than others, be a little more "awake" to their situations, allows me to help those who might feel that they've exhausted their possible solutions.

Now that you know my background and my track record, let's jump into achieving your goals!

I don't know what your aspirations are around your work. I don't know if you aspire to become CEO (or if you already are one), or if you are simply focused on paying the bills. I don't know what problems, individual or organizational, are sitting on your desk or in your mind.

But I know this: the areas I cover here will be relevant to you whether you are a CEO or simply someone who's striving for security.

The following techniques will help you thrive - not just survive - both at the office, and outside of it.

For Starters, Make Time For Work

There's no such thing as an equal division of time between "work" and "life." As long as we're in the workforce, we will be spending the *majority* of our hours performing for our employer, whether self-employed or as an employee.

That's one reason it's so important to love what you do. You can love the challenge, the mission, or the task, but you've got to love some part of it. If you don't, you'll spend most of your work life unhappy.

Later in this book, we'll discuss ways to optimize the *quality* of time you spend outside of work as well to ensure a rich and fulfilling personal life. But for now, let's talk about optimizing your work time.

Time Hack #1: Set Life Expectations Around Your Work Schedule

We might think we are already doing this - but are we, really? Are we planning ahead in a way that works well for everyone, or are we over-committing and disappointing everyone, including ourselves?

Every Sunday, my wife and I sit down with our family and share our week's schedule. We divide and conquer, determining who needs to do what and be where for our jobs and careers. But that's not all we talk about.

We also talk about what we'd like to do outside of work during the week. It's important for our son that we take time to do and talk about this. It's also important to us. And having these discussions from the standpoint of working out the needs of our careers *first* minimizes our frustration.

We let each other know when and where we will physically be during the week. If at least we can't be physically present for each other, we can emotionally and mentally be there for each other, regardless of where we are.

And when we *are* together, we can be completely present, knowing that our time is precious.

Time Hack #2: Make Time Throughout The Day To Check On Family

With smartphones and instant messaging, it's never been easier for us to stay in touch with our families, even when we can't be with them. But how easy is it to forget to do this after we step into the office for the day?

Sending an 'I love you' emoji to your family from work might only take 10 seconds, but the impact could be invaluable.

It's very easy to do and your family is worth it. So set a reminder to check in with your family at least once throughout the day.

This will make a big difference and allows you to be present and attentive in their lives - even when you have to be at work.

Time Hack #3: Make Time to Work From Home, and Even on Vacation

This is a fine line to tread because it requires discipline. On one hand it's easy for the anxious mind to accidentally work or worry about work *all* through your vacation. This can lead to burnout - which results in a long-term loss of productivity.

On the other hand, a disciplined mind knows when it can be productive - and that sometimes the best problem-solving ideas occur when you're out of the office.

With careful management you can reduce your overall workload and stress levels by taking advantage of these peak mental states whenever they occur. You can then be more free to enjoy truly stress-free leisure time knowing that your business has been optimally cared for.

Have you ever come back from a vacation and walked into a storm you weren't prepared for? Many of us end up instantly obliterating the peaceful and joyful state we created for ourselves while we were on vacation. We get hit by a wall of backlogged assignments and problems and we end up ten times more stressed than we were *before* we left for our vacation!

There is a reason why hating Mondays is a grim joke in our culture. Returning to the office after time away can be downright panic-inducing if no one has been keeping an eye on things over the weekend.

Healthy doses of work throughout weekends and vacations, guarded by strong boundaries to ensure you still take truly relaxing personal time, will keep your work muscle healthy and your workload manageable.

It will also allow you to be more present with your family when you aren't working. For example, I purposefully get up at least two hours before my wife gets up on the weekends and on vacation so I can get my work fix in. This leaves us the rest of our day to enjoy together - with even fewer worries since I know exactly what's going on at the office.

Time Hack #4: Be Fully Present To Loved Ones After Work

A few hours per day may not sound like much time to be with your family - but it means the world if you are truly attentive, present, and enjoying them.

Too many working parents do not know how to be fully present with their families, even after work. We become at home zombies because we never shut down our work mentality.

Here's an example of the devastating effect this can have on families:

My Personal Reality Check – Lesson Learned!

My world came to a sudden halt one day when I got home from being on the road. My wife was waiting for me patiently. Somber and quiet, she asked me to sit down and handed me a black book. It was her personal diary. She opened up the page and simply said, 'Read it.'

"What?" I exclaimed!

Tears started flowing down her cheeks. "Read it."

In the book, I read: "Lord, please help me. I no longer know what to do. My own husband, a leader over others, is ignoring me and the family at home. He's physically here, but he's never really here. I have nowhere else to turn. Please help me..."

What a hypocrite I am I thought. Here I am preaching and teaching how to have healthy organizations and I can't even be present for my family. How could I have allowed this to go this far? Something had to change.

Fortunately, something did change.

My trick: I now park my car at the end of the driveway and sit there until I can completely clear my mind of work. Then I think about only one thing: presence. Being fully present for my family once I enter the door of my house.

This has made all the difference in the world!

If you struggle with the ability to "turn off" work thoughts or have anxiety about socializing after a long day at work, it may help to develop a meditation practice.

Meditation is recommended by so many neuroscientists, entrepreneurs, and life hackers for one reason: it really does teach us to regulate our mental and emotional state and allows us to change these states at will.

Discover for yourself what you need to do, mentally or physically, to be fully present for those you love.

Remember: it's not about quantity of time but quality of time.

Money Makes The World Go Round

Most of you probably already hear this a lot, but it bears repeating: money makes the world go round.

One day, I believe we will no longer need money to exchange goods and services. I believe there truly will be equality, liberty and justice for all. Unfortunately however, that *one day* is a long, long way away and probably beyond my lifetime.

Until *that* day, the world will continue to revolve and move via money. As the universal medium of exchange, money is simply the only way of making sure you can get what you need whether you're an individual or an organization.

Fighting this fact will leave you in the dust. However much you might prefer to work for other gains such as service, passion, and fulfillment, money is necessary to ensure you can continue doing what you're doing.

Even churches, monasteries and orphanages need money to operate. Even for nonprofits, making money is the key to survival.

And it's definitely what makes the business world go around. In business, most players are in the game for one reason: to maximize monetary profits. They'll work with whichever employees and organizations allow them to do that.

Money pays our salaries which allow us to secure food and shelter. Money allows companies to pay for their overhead expenses, buy inventory, innovate, optimize and grow.

The instant your organization stops having money, your organization ceases to exist as a viable business.

I'll say it again: regardless of where we work, organizations exist or cease to exist based on their ability to earn and keep money. When shortfalls of money happen, employee layoffs follow.

There are times when companies truly can't afford to keep workers onboard. Then there are extreme times when companies seem to chop heads just to increase their profit margin.

There are times when companies seem to not care at all about the welfare of their people when they appear to be focusing just on profit and nothing else. There are times when people inside of companies get so obsessed with money they start to do unethical or illegal things like embezzle.

While it can sometimes seem hard to understand these more extreme behaviors, it becomes easier when you understand one thing:

Right, wrong or indifferent, making money is the world's certificate of approval. It says whether or not the company is viable and should continue to exist.

Why am I telling you what every business school already teaches? Because I don't want to you take work more *personally* than you need to.

You've heard the old mantra, 'it isn't personal, it's just business.' And you know what? Those who preach that mantra are right! It's just business at the end of the day.

Praise or criticism of your money-making performance are not personal. They're not attacks on your character, self-worth, or overall capabilities. But unfortunately, none of those things are as vital to your ability to make it in business as your money-making ability is.

The only thing that matters in business is *how much money you are bringing in right now* in doing whatever you are currently doing. This can seem like either good news or bad news depending on how we're performing right now.

On one hand, if we're doing well, it certainly keeps us on our toes to know that the market, technology, or other factors might change and our current approach may cease to work.

On the other hand, if we're currently in the red - changing that might be as easy as adopting a new technique or learning a new skill. The importance of money doesn't mean you can't have an enjoyable , fulfilling experience at work. But it does mean that you should keep the importance of making money on the radar screen because it is one of the key metrics of company success

Work relationships are not just about how much a team personally likes you, or what your value or potential is as a human being. They are also about your ability *to contribute to their specific business model* in a way that makes money.

There is *always* a chance that, due to not making *enough* money, your favorite company might have to let you go because they are not able to keep the lights on anymore due to lack of money.

If this ever happens, *don't* take it personally. It's *just* business.

As a consultant, I understand this very clearly. I treat every day as if it could be my last day at the office. The reality is that I'm temporary to my clients in every aspect of the word. Organizations can end my employment without cause at any time.

Two things determine whether I stay or go in these engagements:

1. Am I still adding value?
2. Do they still have budget/money to pay for me?

THE SAME IS TRUE FOR YOU!

Wake up! The reality is that while we are on Earth, it's a dog-eat-dog world. Competition is stiff and automation and artificial intelligence are eliminating many human jobs.

While we can hope that our society will account for this and help prevent these new technologies from causing poverty this trend of increased competition for jobs is *not going away.*

According to Market Watch, artificial intelligence is expected to replace at least 30 million jobs in the next ten to twenty years.[1] This is in addition to millions of jobs lost in previous decades which are not coming back - because they're not needed. Companies are producing more goods and services now than ever before but with fewer workers. The possibility of company extinction is also at an all-time high.

Remember Sears, Toys 'R' Us, and Kmart? These once-indispensable

---

[1] Associated Press. Over 30 million U.S. workers will lose their jobs because of AI. MarketWatch. https://www.marketwatch.com/story/ai-is-set-to-replace-36-million-us-workers-2019-01-24. Published January 24, 2019. Accessed February 1, 2020.

staples of American life became irrelevant as they failed to respond to changes in markets and technologies. The same can happen to us.

Stakeholder demand, whether from publicly held stockholders or privately run boards, requires that we do our very best while they are paying us. This means we must be at the top of our games - individually and organizationally.

These conditions are constant. Change is a constant in the business world. Companies come and go. People come and go. Careers come and go.

Contribute where you can, while you can, because you can.

And remember, *don't* take work more seriously than you need to. It's an important part of life and all of this change can be stressful. But as long as you keep learning and adapting, your career future is under your control.

A particular company or job title's opinion of you is not a reflection on your self-worth or overall capabilities. It certainly doesn't determine whether the rest of your life will be enjoyable or successful.

It's not personal. It's *just* business.

Chapter 2

The People Component

We've discussed the vital role of money in business. But this leaves out the biggest variable that can cause - or resolve - problems in defiance of organizational goals and strategies: people.

Every organization is run by people. Most times this can be a great thing. It's certainly the "human element" of service, camaraderie, contribution and personal meaning that can make workplaces fulfilling for more than just our wallets.

But when the human element is out of alignment work can become hell.

Your boss could be incompetent. Your teammates gossip viciously about each other when backs are turned. Sally-Mae doesn't pull her own weight. Joe Schmoe has to control everything and *everyone!*

These kinds of problems can make us wish we could just *ignore* the human element. But we can't. Not as employees, and certainly not as managers or directors.

Sometimes we probably all agree with David Ramsey, financial guru and radio talk show host: "Business is easy - until people get involved!"

Well guess what? They are *always* involved!

Working with people and their issues is part of the work equation. You *cannot* escape

> Remember, people will *always* be part of the workforce. You *will* have to work with every imaginable personality type. The more skills you can learn to do so without letting strife get under your skin, the more success and peace of mind you will have.

this fact. Businesses often neglect their expertise when it comes to managing people because of the necessity to focus primarily on moving and growing *money,* not relationships or managing emotions. But this can be disastrously costly.

We human beings, with all of our complicated needs and quirks, *are* crazy! Right, wrong or indifferent, this craziness goes with us wherever we go. It even comes with us to the workplace - perhaps *especially* there, where both egos and dollars are involved.

Some of us can hide our quirks for a while but eventually they come out. Others, if they spend time with us·will start to experience and observe them.

We are more *similar* to each other than we are different as human beings. Generally we all want very similar things and are vulnerable to very similar triggers. But *little* differences like the one between you and your colleague have caused World Wars.

There will always be differences in opinion and ways of working in the workplace. We are all unique! We grow up in different environments and have different interpretations of the same formative experiences. We all have different local cultural backgrounds and histories. That in itself *will* cause one person to have behavior that seems "crazy" to another.

These differences between team members can become a source of conflict and strife - or of complementary strengths - depending on how they are handled.

We have two choices *when* apparent "craziness" happens within and around us:

1) Become a victim and contribute to the conflict or
2) Find the most effective way to solve the conflict or at least prevent it from affecting our own work and our work relationships.

Choose option two.

This may feel like it's above your pay grade - after all, you are generally paid for your *business* skills not your people skills. But cultivating these skills can give us a huge advantage in the workforce and make our daily lives a whole lot easier.

What Can I Do When Conflict Arises?

Pay Attention. Stay alert. Be proactive. Do whatever is necessary to remain objective, calm and centered. Align yourself with those in the organization who are *also* choosing option two.

Stay away from those energy-sappers who choose option one. See if help is available. Do what you can to make things better.

In the long run, option one is *not* sustainable. Eventually something will have to change - sometimes in the form of one party leaving the organization. Do your best to make sure that's not you.

You Can Do Everything Right - And Still Get Passed Up

If you are more awake and purposeful than those around you in the workplace, you will be more engaged and responsive. If you are more engaged and responsive, the likelihood that you will win is higher.

Winning feels good! But it is not guaranteed.

You may still find yourself passed up for promotions, or even find your job in danger, *even if you do the "right things."* Changes to markets, technology, workforce, office politics, etc. mean that nothing is ever certain.

Even if you do *all* of the right things, behave in the right way, and work with the right people, there's still a possibility you'll get passed up for the promotion or the raise, be overlooked or even let go.

But remember: don't take it personally. It's just business. In today's highly mobile society, it's increasingly common for companies to let go of employees, and for employees to switch employers. It's more and more common for a person's career game plan to be rendered obsolete and have to change on the fly.

The good news is we're all in the same boat when it comes to this rapid rate of change and unpredictability. Those who are more responsive, awake, and engaged will *still* have a higher chance of winning - because they are more prepared to change their approach and update their skills as the world around them changes in unexpected ways.

Nothing about work operates in a vacuum. Nothing about work is a pure state. It's not just about putting in a required number of hours or checking a set of boxes on your resume that will set you up for life.

Nothing is perfect. Nothing is great all the time or entirely predictable. *All things* are subject to imperfection, mistakes, ups and downs.

Work is no different. There are no guarantees! Ever!

Recognizing the unpredictable nature of the workplace - especially in today's volatile market - can help us avoid the trap of feeling like the "downs" are permanent.

Recognizing that *everyone* must be prepared to change their game plan and that *anyone* could find themselves in trouble due to outside forces can fortify us against the feeling that too many workers fall victim to: that we are failures or are unlikely to ever succeed. That is because our career isn't unfolding according to plan or our future seems hopeless.

No one's career unfolds as planned from day one. Especially not in today's market. Faced with a setback or missed milestone? So what?! So has everyone else at one time or another in their career.

There *are* ways to improve your odds and increase your chances of winning. There are politics, formalities, informalities, and rules of the game for *every* company you become a part of. Familiarize yourself with these, and you'll have an advantage in the game.

Let's thoroughly understand how to do this!

Chapter 3

The CEO Mindset

Not long ago, I was mentoring an aspiring worker of the Millennial generation. He had an undergraduate degree in economics and had recently transitioned from being a teacher to working in the construction business.

At this stage in his life he is still determining his ultimate career path. Does he want to climb the corporate ladder or dedicate his life to public service?

One thing he does know is that he tremendously enjoys helping others to develop themselves and working with small organizations. An ambitious and enterprising individual, he found me via LinkedIn and reached out to me to learn more about what I do in the realm of strategy and organizational leadership.

I told him the importance of being able to hold your own and look anyone you encounter in the eye, regardless of their title or position. Being able to do this commands respect and that sends the signal that you deserve a seat at the table.

"Have you ever been scared or nervous or intimidated by someone's title or position?" he asked me.

"Absolutely," I said. "But they never find that out."

With enough practice in communicating with high-level, high-powered people, you learn to fake it 'til you make it. If you don't manage to fake it - if you look intimidated or out of place - then you get booted out of the room in a millisecond. When it comes to first impressions, confidence is *everything*.

With practice, the intimidation factor goes completely away. You ultimately realize that these intimidating people are simply human beings just like you. No better. No worse.

The *best* way to awaken and start to win is by thinking and acting like a CEO.

Maybe you already *are* the CEO of a company. In that case, we'll use this chapter to brush up on how an ideal CEO *should* act if they wish to grow their company and further advance their career.

Or maybe you're not there yet. Maybe this idea seems scary for you or so far outside of your everyday experience that you don't know where to start.

Don't worry. You already *are* a CEO no matter what your job title is. You are the CEO of your own life.

Aren't you the one who determines where you live, what you wear, what you eat, and how and where you will spend your time and money? Don't you determine how you will live your life, what you will focus on in the coming days, months and years?

Aren't you the maker of your own decisions? Choices? Goals? Strategies? Of course you are. And that gives you a starting point to cultivate the skills of a great CEO.

Whether or not you'd give yourself a good CEO grade for running your life, you *are* doing the job. No one else is going to do it. The only question is, are you a highly effective CEO - or could your executive skills use some work?

This chapter will help you steer your ship effectively and with ease - whether your ship is a billion-dollar company or your own daily life choices.

No matter what your job title or current relationship with work, you *can* achieve "the CEO experience," in which you take charge of your decisions and your destiny. What matters is your mindset, your attitude, your understanding, and actions you take.

When you are proactive in choosing your goals, strategizing and executing your strategy - that's behaving like a CEO. And it will get results regardless of your life stage or job title.

You might be thinking: "But I have a boss who monitors my every move and tells me what to do."

Guess what? CEOs have a boss over them as well. They are called the board members or owners of the company.

No one gets away with *not* having a boss. Everybody reports to *someone* and must strive to meet that person's goals.

Even though I work for myself and run my own firm, I have a boss. At work, it's whoever runs the department or team I'm working with. At home, it's my wife. None of that takes away from my CEO mentality. It's no different from having a company with stakeholders.

When I first joined my Fortune 100 employer, I started at the bottom of the corporate ladder. Despite my already holding a master's degree, the company started me basically at the same level as high school graduates.

Again, I was not advantaged: in fact, I'd had a prior career as a teacher before entering the company and so I was "behind" on the corporate ladder relative to someone who joined straight out of high school.

But I knew that would not determine my destiny. I knew that only my mindset could do that.

My employer had a very traditional process back then. Unless you had an engineering degree that uniquely qualified you for a technical position, you started at the bottom. Even PhDs started at the same level as someone who had a bachelor's degree in engineering. That's just how it was. They did not take my academic experience or my prior work experience into account. They did not take my life experience into account.

For my first five years at my Fortune 100 employer, all of my managers were younger than me. They were all smarter than me when it came to corporate norms: they'd been there longer and knew the company's history, experiences, policies, strategies, etc..

But none of them could touch me with a ten foot pole when it came to my life experience versus theirs. When it came to mindset, they were comparatively inexperienced and immature.

They were accustomed to waiting for orders to be handed down from the top of the ladder, and to being *told* what to do. They were often more concerned with following policies and pleasing immediate supervisors than with getting results.

They were thinking like employees - not like CEOs.

There are some things that you cannot gain just from books or classes. The wisdom you acquire simply by living and making mistakes is one of them. The mindset acquired from being forced to solve problems, from seeing life's ups and downs, and from trial and error is just as valuable as formal education. If not more so.

In my case, I'd been my own CEO since I was orphaned at twelve years old. I had the kind of decision-making experience that comes from having no choice but to take charge of my own destiny.

So I didn't let my bottom-of-the-ladder position at the company stop me from being my own CEO and pushing the limits. I did research and learned new skills without being told to do so. I let my self-study be guided by my sense of how to get results, not based on the rules or expectations I'd been given by my supervisors.

I met those too, of course - but I also went above and beyond. Not to impress anybody or compete for a promotion, but simply to improve my own results and those of my department.

Soon, upper management at the company noticed my attitude, my mindset, my initiative, sense of responsibility, and my results. I was continually promoted to higher positions. After several years I reached a point where I gained autonomy

> **Who you are as CEO - how you incorporate the CEO mindset into your life - determines your results. Not your job title, your boss, your paycheck, or even your formal education!**

and oversaw the consumer research and development of a North American product division.

At this point, my bosses were all in Europe. I had effectively surpassed the American chain of command.

At the same time I was able to create bandwidth for myself and became part of the Asian Pacific American Steering Committee, joined the corporate training arm of the company teaching classes on leadership, got my second master's degree, and developed a new leadership program within my department.

This didn't happen because I had a superhuman IQ, or came from a billionaire family, or didn't need to sleep. It happened because I was consistent in making decisions based on ambition and on strategy.

By running my own life like a CEO - constantly monitoring my results, holding myself to deadlines, and refining my methods to create improvements - I got more results than anyone in the company who was simply following orders and doing what they were told.

Outside of work, I bought and sold real-estate, taught martial arts, got my executive coaching certification, taught financial and leadership programs at my church, and spent time with my family.

This was a result of acting as the CEO of my own life. I didn't leave my strategic optimizing mindset at the office when I left work for the day!

Who you are as a CEO - how you incorporate the CEO mindset into your life - determines your results. Not your job title, your boss, your paycheck, or even your formal education!

You'll still have to navigate the conditions, situations, politics, rules of the game, the culture, and just the 'unfairness' of work that might sometimes be against you.

But don't let that stop you. When you realize that your destiny is in your own hands and adopt the CEO mindset, you begin to see results. Not, as my story illustrates, when you have perfect conditions and every advantage in your favor.

"Perfect conditions" don't exist. Even if they did - you wouldn't want them!

Not when smooth sailing often means losing your edge and allowing others to decide your destiny for you, instead of deciding it for yourself.

Steps To The CEO Mindset

I challenge you to act as if you were the CEO of your workplace - and your life - with every challenge and decision that arises.

For massive success, consider incorporating the following cornerstones of the CEO mindset into your daily life:

Step 1: Treat company money like your own and try to make more of it!

My executive MBA professor of digital transformation gave us a simple challenge around company money: Try to make your company contribution equal to ten times your salary.

What does this mean, and how do you do it?

No matter your role, whether it be technical or business-related, do what you can to contribute ten times back what the company invests in you in terms of pay. This will ensure you are a valuable asset wherever you go - whether you want to switch employers, angle for a promotion, or begin working for yourself eventually.

If you are making a $100,000 a year, see what you can do to somehow generate $1 million back in terms of value. See what you can do to optimize cost savings, sales, and any other factor in company cash flow that you might have influence over.

How *differently* might you act if company money were really *your* money?

Would you have the same propensity to spend like you do on travel expenses? What about approving head count? Raises? How differently would you treat your budget if you acted as if it were literally coming out of your checkbook?

Would you spend more time outside the office learning new skills to increase your return on investment? How hard would you work to multiply your own paycheck ten times?

How do you treat your budget when you run out of money? Do you ask for more? Do you borrow from the future? Or do you figure out how to generate more money yourself?

Treating company money like it's your money helps you take more ownership of your spending and ensures that you can generate reliable return on investment (ROI).

It also prepares you to start thinking about your own money as business revenue that can be used efficiently - or poorly.

What can you do to maximize return on investment in your own life in terms of your empowerment, fulfillment, and ultimate life goals?

When you know the answer to that, you're on the path to financial health *and* life fulfillment.

Step 2: Ask what's best for the company first, instead of what is best for you.

Objectivity is the goal here. How can you evaluate your own performance and value to a company the way your boss or CEO would?

When you think this way, sometimes self-preservation needs to become the second priority.

Being able to generate huge value for a business and make the decisions that are best for it will pay off more in the long run than enjoying a slightly easier life at the expense of your company. Cultivating this objective evaluation of "what is best for the company" will make you a more valuable asset to future employers and a more successful CEO or business owner in your own right.

Let me tell you a story that perfectly illustrates the company-first mindset - and its often unexpected benefits.

A CEO once asked me to help remove him from his position. He believed he had reached his limit in terms of his ability to help his company grow. He believed he had reached his leadership ceiling and was not the best person to serve the company moving forward.

Thinking of the company, not himself, he prepared to resign from his prestigious position and called me in to ensure that he did the best job possible handling the hand-off and training his replacement.

But I knew an invaluable CEO when I saw one. The very

company-first mindset that had him considering resigning made him the best leader the company could have asked for. He simply needed to upgrade his skills and his confidence.

So instead of helping him resign, I helped him grow. It turned out that this CEO only needed to reformulate his vision and strategies for the company, and acquire some new skills to allow him to execute a bigger, bolder strategy than ever before.

His glidepath - and the growth of the company - is limitless now.

This CEO truly had the company-first mindset. He thought of what was best for the company always - *before* thinking about his individual prestige or comfort. And that is why he ultimately succeeded.

I've worked with many individuals who treat the company simply as a paycheck and nothing else. In this scenario, no one wins. The company suffers from apathetic workers and leaders - and the workers and leaders lose out on developing skills that could increase their value in the marketplace exponentially.

I am all for taking care of you. Self-care - in the sense of making sure one has a truly fulfilling and nourishing personal life - is vital to all things.

But an apathetic approach which seeks to achieve comfort with minimal effort does not help on *either* front. Instead, the characteristic of putting forth effort to optimize, strategize, and achieve generalizes to *both* areas of life - if you don't exercise optimization at work, you're likely not exercising it in your personal life either.

In addition to optimizing, strategizing, and achieving, you want to be *recognized* for your achievements. You want others to be able to look at you and see that you are a proactive problem-solver and innovator who brings serious value to everything you do.

In order to ensure that others see your value, you must…

Step 3: Carry Yourself Like A CEO

What do you think I mean when I say "carry yourself like a CEO?" What do you picture in your mind when you imagine how a CEO conducts themselves in a meeting or on the street?

Carrying yourself like a CEO does not mean being arrogant and pompous. If anything, that's the sign of a CEO who's not very good at their job. That's someone who's more caught up in their personal importance than in the well-being of their company and workers.

Ideal CEOs are confident, poised, and act like they belong in the room. They are confident that the skills they have are powerful and bring tremendous value. But they *also* accord the respect of equals to other people in the room.

If they don't recognize the potential value of others' contributions after all, how can they be sure they have all the information they need to make the best decisions for their company?

The key word here is "equals." When you are stepping into a boardroom, you must do so with the knowledge that you belong there as someone who offers tremendous value. Regardless of the title, paycheck, or seniority of the others in the room, you must tell them with your body language that you have something of value to offer them.

But you must *not* act as though you are *more* important than the other people in the room. That betrays naivete at best. At worst, it suggests you might not care about the outcomes experienced by other members of your team or might be too short-sighted to listen to important information from them.

So carry yourself with both confidence *and* respect for others. These are the marks of a truly great CEO.

Here's a fun exercise: The next time you go into a public setting, like a restaurant, see if you can *size up* the room and determine who carries themselves with confidence, poise and respect.

You may be surprised to find how much you can deduce about the job titles, paychecks, and social status of the people in the room - just by observing the way they move and interact with each other.

Now how can you emulate those with the most prestigious job titles? How can you carry yourself like someone who *deserves* to be given command of that big project, because you know you have the skills to pull it off?

Confidence and skill form a happy feedback loop for the ambitious current or aspiring CEO. The more you are able to carry yourself like a confident and skilled individual, the more confident you will be in your ability to perfect new skills. And the more you invest in rising to the challenge of those skills - the more capable you will become.

True confidence is never blind. True confidence comes from *learning through experience* that you can do it, by subjecting yourself to hard tests and constantly improving your performance.

That's why, to achieve true boardroom-level mastery, you must...

Step 4: Hold Yourself Accountable Like A CEO

This is the part of being a CEO that the general public never sees. Many people think of CEOs as fabulously powerful people who never experience a moment of discomfort or blame.

However, nothing could be further from the truth. The truth is, CEOs face more pressure to perform than anyone else. You only get a company to give you that job title in the first place by taking an extreme amount of responsibility for your own performance.

After all, the flip side of power is responsibility. A CEO can blame anyone in their company for a mistake or problem - *but that won't fix the problem.* The only way for a CEO to actually *fix* a problem is to take responsibility for the problem, and hold themselves accountable for the decisions that created it.

There is not one role I know in a company that comes with as much pressure to perform and deliver than the CEO position. Truly being CEO of a company is a tall order that requires you have the gumption and courage to *fill the shoes*, no matter what size they might be.

Candidly, not everyone is cut out for the position. Those who prefer jobs they can "leave at the office" outside of the 9-5 might not find the trade-off of responsibility for power to be worth it.

To become a CEO, you have to be willing to subject yourself to the fire on a daily basis, both from inside and outside company. You have to be willing to put yourself out there and be subject to both criticism and praise. When times are good, you get the credit. When times are bad, you get the brunt of the blame.

The truth is, no one person should have to carry the brunt of that weight. We should all hold ourselves accountable for our performance and our department's performance, no matter what our job title is.

And that's not just good for our company and our CEO. It's also good for *us*.

Only by taking responsibility like a CEO - by behaving with the knowledge that *no one can solve the problem but us* - can we create in ourselves the kind of high-performance mentality that leads to great personal power.

When we own both the good and the bad results of our actions, we own our power. That means we must also own the criticism we receive and constantly consider how we can improve.

That's what accountability is. And that's how you get power.

Of course, no person is an island. *Everyone* must communicate with others in order to do their jobs and advance in their careers. Whether it's colleagues, clients, bosses, or oversight authorities - how others respond to us is a big factor in determining what we can achieve.

That's why you must also...

Step 5: Communicate Like a CEO

How do people usually feel after they get done talking to you? The answer to this question says a great deal about your career path, your quality of life at home, and even your odds of getting a promotion.

Do you inspire with your messages? Can most recipients understand what you are communicating? Do people respond swiftly and correctly to your requests and orders?

Or are you in the weeds in your communication? Do people often forget or misunderstand your requests? Do they seem reluctant or irritated to comply with them?

Here is a great place to hold yourself accountable like a CEO.

Instead of blaming others when you don't get the outcome you'd prefer from a communication, consider how you could make your communications more clear and more inspiring.

Remember - people are more likely to fulfill a request or order quickly if they feel great about doing it.

No CEO or human being has perfect communication skills. We all make mistakes and can find ways to improve.

Highly effective CEOs operate under the principle that *less is more* when it comes to communication. Two or three sentences should be all it takes to create a clear understanding or request.

A good CEO can relate to you on the person -to -person front and connect with you - but also knows how to get down to business when it 's time to do the work . They hold you to the same high standards as they hold themselves.

Frequent reminders or long paragraphs of text shouldn't be necessary. Not only are those time-consuming; they can actually reduce the recipient's understanding and motivation.

Believe me - you would feel that "less is more," too, if you had over a thousand things to occupy your space like a typical CEO does!

CEO-like communication is not only about content, but also about projection. What impression do you give in your written communications?

Just like the way you yourself in-person, your communication must project presence, clarity, confidence and competence.

Step 6: Treat Others The Way A Great CEO Would

Successful CEOs treat other people very much like they treat themselves. They treat their people with respect and ensure they have everything they need to perform well and lead rewarding lives. But they also hold employees to a high standard of accountability for their results and deliverables.

A good CEO can relate to you on the person -to-person front and connect with you - but also knows how to get down to business when it's time to do the work. They hold you to the same high standards as they hold themselves. They won't let how much they like you or want to support you cloud their business judgement, anymore than they'll let their own desires cloud their judgement about their own performance.

If you can do both - treat people the way you would want to be treated, in both compassion and accountability - you will not only be respected as a leader in your role, but also as a relatable and admirable person.

Some of you might still be thinking: *I don't care about ever becoming a CEO, let alone acting like one.*

But remember: the traits that make a great CEO are desired for a reason. These are the traits that allow you to make *anything* happen - whether it's transformative community service, a rich and rewarding personal life, or a quarter of record-breaking business growth.

I would argue that if anyone is to be truly happy, he must be CEO of his life. He must hold himself accountable for the things that go wrong - and in so doing, take the staggering power to make things go *right* into his own hands.

This includes work performance, whether it's climbing the corporate ladder or just paying the bills in the most fulfilling way possible.

At the very least, if someone wishes to be successful, he must not put his personal satisfaction in someone else's hands. He must own it himself. That's the essence of what becoming your own CEO is all about.

Do it the right way and everyone wins: you, your people, and the company where you work. So make a commitment to *always* be the CEO of your life and work, regardless of what goals or job titles you might have.

Your self-worth and personal power will thank you for it!

Chapter 4

The Power of Your Mission

You may have noticed something about all of the characteristics of the CEO Mindset discussed in the last chapter: *They are all goal-oriented.*

"Competence" and "effectiveness," have no meaning unless you're talking about one's competence or effectiveness at *achieving a specific goal.*

> *If you can't get behind your company's mission statement, you might as well find somewhere else to work*

Are you behind your organization's cause? Do you believe in the reason it exists? Does what it does or what it makes inspire you?

If you can't get behind your company's mission statement you are already set up for failure and will most assuredly remain *asleep and not fully engaged* at work. After all, a paycheck is just a paycheck. All the dollars and job titles in the world won't motivate employees or leaders the way a powerful *mission* will.

Ever go to an event or a movie you had *no interest* in and sat through it for your spouse or your friends? What happened when you got there?

We both know the answer to this. If it was a movie, I can almost guarantee that you fell asleep. If it was an event, you *definitely* were just going through the motions.

Work is no different! You must be able to get behind your company's mission or you won't be able to perform as a great CEO.

We humans *must* have a sense of purpose to everything we do. We're not innately motivated by numbers in a bank account. We're motivated by making the world a better place. To do that, we'll go above and beyond the call of duty. But if we feel like our work is *not* doing that - then high-level performance is not sustainable in the long run.

Understanding your company's mission statement is a first step toward achieving that sense of purpose. If you're a CEO, creating a great mission statement and ensuring that your employees appreciate their role in it is the first step toward great organizational performance.

If you can't get behind your company's mission statement, you might as well find somewhere else to work. If you're honest with yourself, you know you're already half checked-out anyway.

If you're a CEO whose employees don't know, support, or feel connected to your company's mission - chances are they are half checked-out too.

Mission statements are the lighthouse of the organization. They guide all of the company's strategic decisions and daily actions.

Not having a mission statement is similar to being a wanderer on Earth. You will have no sense of direction. You can't measure your effectiveness or improve it if you don't know what you're

> **A mission statement is the company's purpose, the reason it exists.**

trying to achieve in the world. With no sense of direction, you will end up *anywhere or nowhere.*

For an example of a highly successful company's mission statement, here is Amazon's:

Mission: "We strive to offer our customers the lowest possible prices, the best available selection, and the utmost convenience."[2]

As of 2019, Amazon online sales accounted for 38% of *all* U.S. online sales.[3] That means people chose to do business with Amazon as often as they chose *all competing companies combined.* I'd say

---

[2] https://mission-statement.com/amazon/

[3] https://www.pymnts.com/amazon/2019/amazon-share-ecommerce/

that Amazon has done a pretty stellar job of getting behind their mission statement!

So what exactly *is* a mission statement? And how do you make a great one?

A Google search will tell you that a mission statement is a formal summary of the aims and values of a company, organization, or individual.

A mission statement is the company's purpose, the reason it exists.

It's not a financial goal. Finances are your company's gas tank. Instead of asking "how do we fill the gas tank," ask: "Why are we on this drive in the first place? Why take this road, instead of any other? What unique value are we trying to create?"

Ideally, a mission statement is not finite but should live beyond any individual or technology. A great mission statement speaks to meeting a need so deep and universal that the mission should never have to change, no matter how much the outside world changes.

One of the companies I've been privileged to work with for over a decade has the following mission statement:

"To relentlessly protect people, property and the environment."

That's a need that will never go away. There will always be people, property, and environments, and there will always be dangers that threaten them. This company can keep its sights set on its true purpose for existence rather than getting hung up on the specific technologies or methods it currently uses.

Currently, this company focuses on providing fire suppression and the protection of data centers and oil refineries, as well as providing manufacturing sites with personal protective equipment. In the future, the company might focus on cyber-protection or the protection of space stations and orbital mining operations.

Regardless of what happens to technology or the market, their mission statement will still be relevant. That means they'll always be focused on what's important, and nothing will change the world so radically that they can't adapt to it through proper management.

My questions for you are:

- Do you know your company's mission statement?
- Is it still relevant for you?
- Do you still believe in it?
- Are your company's operations fully aligned to its mission?

If you answered "yes" to all the above, you have taken the first step in the awakening process at work. You believe in what you do beyond just the goal of obtaining power or a paycheck. Because you are dedicated to accomplishing your company's purpose, you can innovate and excel in the service of making that happen.

If you answered "no," it might be time to revisit your "why" and either get yourself aligned to your company's mission or leave for a place you believe in.

When starting with new companies or teams, I ask them if they know their company's mission statement. Sometimes I get blank stares. Other times I get simple nods. Sometimes I get lots of passion and energy from them.

Guess which companies perform the best, financially speaking, and are least likely to go out of business?

If you guessed the enthusiastic teams, you're right!

Centering on the mission statement *first*, especially for new engagements or if your company hasn't visited it for a while, is a great way to recalibrate folks as to why you are doing what you are doing and how you make the world a better place.

When times are tough or your company has to make tough calls, it is easy to lose sight of your "why." And if you lose sight of your "why," you're almost guaranteed not to make the best decision.

The *most* important why of your company is your mission. Why does this company exist in the first place? What purpose does it exist to achieve?

Out of your mission comes your vision. And out of your vision come your strategies, core competencies, goals, milestones, - all the tools you need for success.

Everything your company needs to succeed is derived first and foremost from your mission!

Chapter 5

Your Vision

While a mission ideally *shouldn't* change with time, your vision should. This is because your vision - what you are capable of, and what is needed in the marketplace - will change over time.

I often ask teams who are developing their vision: "When should we change our vision?"

Eventually, I get one daring participant to answer: "When we've finally achieved our vision, and it's no longer aspirational."

That explanation is both true and incomplete.

You see, your vision may describe your company's ideal state. It may meet all of your company's needs both short term and long term. In that case, you wouldn't need to change your vision when it is accomplished.

An example of this is the following vision that I helped a church develop:

"To be a thriving family center of spiritual leaders where congregants are joyfully and actively involved, influencing beyond our center, and the center is financially healthy and steadily growing."

For this organization, simply being able to maintain this vision was their goal. Being a nonprofit and debt-free, the above vision statement met their needs because it had everything that they needed to be considered to be thriving:

- Active and joyful congregants
- Influencing beyond their center

- Financially healthy
- Steadily growing

The descriptions were clear, the targets were clear, and the areas of focus were clear. All in all, their vision was clear. But it wasn't limiting.

Note that their vision didn't make any statements about the size, shape, technology, or scope of the organization. It only mandated joy, influence, financial health, and constant growth.

This was a church that had been around for over seventy years prior to this vision - and when I met them, they were badly in need of a vision update.

Prior to establishing this vision, the church was not healthy in the above areas. They were operating on old ideas of what a church "should" be and what a church "should" do, and they weren't thriving. They had joyful congregants for sure, but there wasn't a focus on growth, finances, or strategies to influence the wider community beyond their church walls.

> If your company's mission is its lighthouse that always guides the way, describing the purpose of your organization's existence, **the vision is its road map or GPS route**.

Establishing a new vision allowed this organization to unleash those previously neglected potentials within itself. If your company's mission is its lighthouse that always guides the way, describing the purpose of your organization's existence, the vision is its road map or GPS route.

Without the vision, companies tend to wing it. They don't have a clear sense of what priorities they must focus on to achieve their mission. Without a clear vision statement, it is impossible to create strategies and priorities for your company in an optimal way.

Without the vision, you'll be stuck in the day-to-day. You'll have a vague sense that you're probably getting closer to the lighthouse but you won't know if you're on the safest or shortest route.

Without the vision, your company won't properly *stretch* and *grow*. The vision allows you to aspire and challenge your company - in the ways that are *most important to your mission*.

Your vision is what you'd like to see your organization become in the short-to-medium term. It's where you'd like your company to be five years from now.

Your vision is what will start to put your company into action mode. It will be based on an evaluation of where your company has been, where it is today, and where you'd like it to be tomorrow.

If there is *ever* a place to *reset* your entire company, it is in the creation of your *vision*. This shared vision is what your employees will work together every day to create. Changing *anywhere* else, *if* your vision is not set, owned and bought into, will just feel like you are plugging leaks and putting Band-Aids on a machine that's in need of a full overhaul.

The same is true for your personal development. Developing a *vision* of who you want to be in three months, one year, or five years will keep you on-target in becoming who you want to be.

Let's look at some examples of how updates to a company's vision can allow the company to thrive despite drastically changing times.

- IBM used to put together computers installed with Microsoft software and sell them.[4] Once hardware clones flooded the market, they were drastically losing market share. They shifted into becoming known for being IT experts - and doing that better than anyone else on the market - instead.
- Berkshire Hathaway, Warren Buffet's company, was initially a textile company in the early 1960s.[5] He sold the textile business off completely due to foreign competition and converted it to a holding company, performing a completely different function from its initial success. The rest is history.
- In the early 1800s, Marcus Samuel first started what we know today as Shell Oil. Back then, he and his family *actually*

---

[4] https://www.ibm.com/ibm/history/history/history_intro.html
[5] https://www.britannica.com/topic/Berkshire-Hathaway

sold shells and eventually expanded into a global import and export business. Once the oil boom hit in the late 19th century, the Samuels built the first bulk oil tanker as a natural expansion of its import/export business model.[6]

- Before the first Nintendo Entertainment System came out in 1985, Nintendo Koppai was a playing card company way back in 1889. Time and time again, Nintendo has continued to redefine itself as technology has changed the ways people consume entertainment.[7]

- Back in 1848, American Express was part of the *Pony Express,* and transported both packages and currency from the East Coast to the West. They came up with the world's first travelers checks as a new way of transferring money over long distances or while traveling, and are known today as a leading global financial services and travel company.[8]

The above examples show that with a powerful vision, *anything* is possible! A company's business model, technology, and marketplace can completely change - all while the company still achieves enormous success thanks to a vision which responds to the changing times.

Some of these companies started back in the 1800s. They are still around today - and are leading the world in industries that did not even exist when they were founded.

Remember Toys 'R' Us, once the number-one toy retail department store in the nation? It has closed its doors because it was unable to compete with Amazon and its ecommerce and distribution platform.

We're talking about a company that once was a multi-billion dollar organization - but they failed to adapt to technological and market changes.

Let's look at why that might be:

---

[6] https://www.shell.com/about-us/our-heritage/our-company-history.html
[7] https://www.nintendo.co.uk/Corporate/Nintendo-History/Nintendo-History-625945.html#1889
[8] https://about.americanexpress.com/our-history

Toys "R" Us Mission Statement: "Our Goal is to be the Worldwide Authority on Kids, Families and Fun."

Toys "R" Us Vision Statement: "Our Vision is to put joy in kids' hearts and a smile on parents' faces."[9]

What do you see missing from their vision statement?

Remember, a vision statement's job is to be *more specific* than a mission statement.

Toys "R" Us' vision statement might have been a great mission statement, but it says nothing about how, specifically, they planned to create and cultivate happy customers, or cultivate their infrastructure or influence to meet the needs of a changing market.

What would you have added, if you had been in charge of this company? When would you have updated its vision statement, and how?

Toys "R" Us is not unique in today's climate. Many billion-dollar household brand names have gone down as consumer buying habits and successful business models have radically shifted. Others - like the early examples - have survived even more radical changes in their organizational lifetimes, and are still on top today.

Companies that can't harmonize their vision with the market, change, and be agile may become extinct overnight. This is always true, at any point in history.

It could be today's e-commerce, digital revolution, or yesterday's industrial revolution. Perhaps the future will hold a brain/computer interface revolution, an artificial intelligence revolution, or some similarly radical change to how goods are produced, purchased, and distributed.

An agile company need not fear. If you can master a mission statement that will never become obsolete and support that mission with a vision that updates to suit the changing times, you may become

---

[9] http://www.makingafortune.biz/list-of-companies-t/toys-r-us.html

the next Shell Oil, formerly Shell Imports - or American Express, formerly part of the Pony Express.

A healthy organization must continually review, revise and restructure to remain relevant. That means revisiting, returning to, and revising their mission, vision and values with reckless enthusiasm.

We can never become complacent around our mission and vision. The moment we become comfortable with success, we lose touch with reality.

Vision Pitfalls to Avoid

If you want to see your vision fulfilled, you must ensure *none* of the below pitfalls are occurring. I know this because I have personally witnessed each of them at one time another. These organizations were only able to be saved by addressing their vision problems with experience and expertise in a timely fashion.

Many other organizations have not been so lucky - they have not caught these problems in time.

Do yourself and your company a huge favor by familiarizing yourself with these pitfalls - and taking proactive measures to avoid them:

Problem 1: Your Vision Isn't Aligned With Your Mission

Yes, believe it or not, this can happen. Companies can lose sight of their foundational purpose, or mission, or values.

Before they know it, the vision completely veers away from their "why." They end up performing actions that aren't consistent with their core competencies or their customer base, expending budget with little to no return on investment in either worker satisfaction or consumer dollars.

In some cases, the forest of mission is lost in the trees of the marketplace. It's easy to go down the three-door rabbit hole of meeting customer needs, keeping up with competition and appeasing the stockholders.

But these individual actions taken to solve individual problems miss the big picture. The parts no longer work harmoniously and strategically together, and new problems begin to appear even more quickly than they are solved.

Remember GE? Recently, they became heavily involved in banking and subprime loans. What seemed like a good idea in the short term did not take advantage of their core competencies such as aviation, product engineering and energy. Now, they are struggling to stay afloat.[10]

Problem 2: Your Vision Is Too Far From Your Current State

You might think that aiming for the stars with your vision is great. But there's a problem with this: if your vision can't be achieved by your team in 2-3 years, there's a good chance it won't be achieved *at all*.

Today's world is ten-fold more competitive than the market of the last century, thanks to globalization and constantly evolving technology. New companies crop up daily, especially those based on digital platforms. Some of these have huge advantages, precisely because they *are* new - and therefore have the expertise and agility to master the latest market trends and technological tools.

Changing and evolving slowly is no longer an option. Instead of a five-to-ten year plan, consider a two-to-three year vision. Visions with a more limited, shorter timeline are *much* more beneficial for driving a sense of urgency and making decisions. Shorter time frames allow better measurement, and minimize missed opportunities.

Shorter time frames also allow the organization to pivot and change more rapidly - often an essential for success in this global information age.

Being agile is the new norm, and is more important to success than ever before.

Problem 3: Your Vision Is Too Abstract

It's important to inspire your employees and your board with big, ambitious ideas and heartfelt values. But some vision statements are *so* broad and nebulous that they tell a company little about how to direct its daily activities to meet those lofty goals.

Remember the Toys "R" Us vision statement? It said *nothing*

---

[10] https://fortune.com/longform/ge-decline-what-the-hell-happened/

about how to measure customer satisfaction, cultivate market-relevant core competencies, or seek to influence the larger culture and market.

You might as well be dreaming. You've created a lovely vision of reality - but you haven't determined any steps to get there. Or at least, you haven't managed to communicate those to the team that will be executing your vision.

Problem 4: Your Vision Is Not Integrated Throughout Your Organization

If you want to know how organizations naturally get morphed into unhealthy silos that suffer from lack of cooperation and communication, look no further than the vision statement. Too many people in organizations get caught up in being cooks in their own kitchen.

It's natural for different departments to have their own ideas about a company's vision statement. After all, they have different areas of expertise, and the way we address a problem varies according to what tools we have.

But when this natural process is allowed to continue without intervention, the results can be disastrous. Departmental interpretations of the company's mission might vary so widely that leaders within the company begin to fight over the best way to implement the company's vision, with little regard for data from other departments.

For this reason, it's essential to have sufficient communication to keep *all* departments focused on the big picture - and even allow them to compare notes so they can see their own place in the larger plan.

If this doesn't happen, departmental operations can become misaligned or even actively conflict.

Problem 5: Your Vision Is Not Sufficiently Challenged Or Revisited

As I write this section , my former Fortune 100 femployer is going through some challenging times, both financially and with its people. They are experiencing high turnover and company valuation is volatile.

This is *not* normal for this company, as they have traditionally experienced extensive stability and growth for more than 150 years! Turbulent times are a signal that it might be time to challenge your vision statement in order to discover the root of this turmoil. When you find the root of the problem, you will have found its solution.

Problem 6: Your Vision Is Misaligned With Your Core Competencies

This means you are trying to be who you are not. Have you ever walked into a gas station that served prime rib? Or how about a golf course that tries to be a polo club, with actual horses?

Such a business would have obvious problems. It would be investing huge amounts of resources in trying to do something that it frankly wasn't very good at. This would lead to massive inefficiency due to lack of expertise and even physical infrastructure and maybe catastrophic failure.

Are you putting your effort into doing the jobs you're best at? Or have your strongest skills been left out of your vision?

Problem 7: You Fail To Execute Your Vision

In their book, *The Balanced Scorecard*, authors David Norton and Robert Kaplan note that **90 percent of organizations fail to execute on their vision successfully.**[11]

Wow! This is an alarming and dismal statistic. But it's not surprising.

I see this every day in practice. Good, solid companies investing countless hours, research dollars and resources, in developing a strategic plan to achieve the vision...only to find at the end of the year that practical, business, and personnel barriers prevented successful execution.

---

[11] Kaplan RS, Norton DP. *The Balanced Scorecard: Translating Strategy Into Action*. Boston, MA: Harvard Business School Press

If we pay close attention, we know the list of excuses is endless. But here are some of the most common – and truly formidable – barriers that get in the way of making our strategic visions a reality:

Problem 8: You Get Caught Up In Daily "Urgent" Tasks

Have you ever said to yourself: "I have too much on my plate just putting out fires and avoid falling behind. I don't have time to worry about the company's vision and growth goals."

That's a very easy thing to feel. Let's face it, the *now* is more pressing than the future.

Fulfilling a vision requires disciplined movement toward the vision, making it a priority. This is something overwhelmed leaders often choose to put off for another day.

Leaders can help with this by encouraging or *requiring* regular time investments in the company's vision. But those without foresight often neglect to do this, choosing to take the short-term gain of a few hours per week at the expense of the long-term gain of upgraded company-wide abilities.

Don't be one of those business leaders without foresight. Recognize the value of consistently carving out time for long-term investment, even if you feel that you don't have the time to spare.

Problem 9: You Spend All Your Time Putting Out Fires

We often allow ourselves and others to become distracted from pursuing our organization's vision by short-term stressors. A burning building or acute crisis always takes precedence because it's happening *now*.

Often, this is a failure to distinguish between "urgent" and "important." Nothing will ever be perfect and less than ideal events will always happen.

Just because someone is demanding a solution *now* or some less-than-ideal thing has happened, doesn't necessarily mean that this "crisis" takes precedence over fulfilling the company's long-term vision.

It takes discipline to say "actually, this may not be the highest priority" when there's always *something* that could be fixed or optimized somewhere in your company or department.

Problem 10: You Don't Consciously Choose Your Daily Priorities

Which of your ten top priorities is your number-one priority today?

Coming up with ideas for priorities is *not* a problem. You can probably think of at least a dozen things you'd "like to prioritize" today.

Acting on your priorities *is* a problem for most of us. And it's whether we act on our priorities on a daily basis that determines whether we will accomplish them.

Did you choose how to spend your time today consciously and strategically based on what will most advance your long-term goals? Or did you just pick up the first e-mail or piece of paper that someone dropped on your desk?

What success criteria are you using to determine which priority is *most* important for you to act on daily?

Are you taking long-term growth and optimization into account in your daily choices, or focusing only on what is immediate, easy, and convenient?

If you don't consciously prioritize the most important tasks and *make* time for these tasks before others, they simply won't get done.

When you're in the business world, you never get to the bottom of your to-do list.

So you'd better make sure that the most important things are at the top of your to-do list each day.

Problem 11: You Have The Wrong People On The Bus or They're in the Wrong Seat

Are we clear on who needs to do what? Are we clear on who owns what? Is our team meeting their milestones? If not, why not?

Does someone need more support or guidance - or do they lack enthusiasm or competency to complete their part of the plan?

Would one or a few of your people be more enthusiastic or competent in a different seat, or on a different bus?

Or are most team members having problems performing - suggesting that the bus driver, the company practices, or some other common denominator might be the problem?

It can feel difficult to address problems of low performance, or to suggest a change of team responsibilities for someone. But if their core competencies and passions aren't aligned with the project and they're not producing results, trying to fit a square peg into a round hole won't make anyone happy.

Problem 12: You Don't Have Clear Metrics, Goals, Or Timelines

To make sure that progress is happening, all progress must be measurable. There must be concrete, measurable goals to which you can definitively say "yes, this has been accomplished," or "no, it hasn't been."

This might be a checklist of tasks to accomplish, a financial goal, the results of a survey or skill test, or something else.

You should also have a concrete *timeline*. Set a deadline for your results to be achieved. Were they achieved?

If yes, congratulations! Now, what's your next concrete goal?

If not, *why* not?

Is there something wrong with your goal, its measurement, or your plan to improve it? If so, it's better to find out sooner - at an established, concrete deadline - than later, after a huge amount of time has elapsed without success.

The important thing is that your goal is *measurable*.

Your optimization is not dependent on someone's opinion of how they *think* or *feel* about progress but on demonstrable results you can use to determine exactly how close you are to achieving your vision.

Problem 13: No One Is Holding You Accountable For The Vision

This is related to the last pitfall. Successful execution of goals requires three things:

1. Measurable, concrete goals, so you can know with certainty whether or not they have been achieved.
2. Firm, regular deadlines at which assessments are conducted to see if goals have been met.
3. *Action is taken* if goals are not met.

Inquiries into "why" are conducted. Plans are re-formulated. The skills and performance of those responsible for the goal are evaluated. Rewards or penalties are assigned if helpful. The best solution to advancing the goal is found.

This is accountability.

It doesn't mean simply blaming the people who have not met the goal. Jumping to blaming individuals can be worse than useless to the company's long-term goals if the root of the problem turns out to be the company's policies, technology, training programs, or support resources. You can absolutely guarantee you won't fix a thing if you don't realize something is wrong with it.

True accountability is when organizational leadership takes responsibility for missed goals, and does whatever it takes to determine how best to move their company forward. It can also mean *rewarding* those who do meet goals or who find important problems that need to be solved.

In today's fast-paced business world, it's easier to reward those who put out fires than those who make contributions to fulfilling the company's vision that will pay off handsomely in the long term.

We need to reward those who hold us accountable for plowing

ahead with our vision, even in a world where there are always fires and less-than-ideal happenings that need to be addressed.

Problem 14: Your Vision Outlasts Your Leadership

When leadership turnover occurs, it can be easy for the new leaders to not fully understand, or be fully invested in the organization's vision.

This might occur because the vision actually needs to be updated to reflect current marketplace realities. In this case, that update shouldn't be neglected: an outdated vision can sink a whole company, like Toys "R" Us.

On the other hand, it might occur as a result of insufficient education of the new leaders. Always make sure that your leaders - or you *as* a leader - are onboard with the company's vision.

If leadership and vision are not in alignment, that's a certain sign that *one* of them needs to change their tune for optimal company success.

Problem 15: There Is No Process In Place To Achieve Your Vision

My SAOL Vision Continuum (below) hits on key points. Which of these points are most important for *your* company will depend on which steps you have already completed to a high standard, and what your company's acute needs and weak points are.

Regardless of the process you choose to follow, know that fulfilling a vision takes at least eighteen to twenty-four months. In many cases it can be even longer - but you shouldn't let it go for more than thirty-six months in today's fast-paced, rapidly changing market.

So take a look at this road map, and decide where your organization currently is along this path:

1. **It all starts with solidifying your vision:** The vision provides a sense of direction for employees and serves as a compass

for your business' activities. Create your vision at the highest level of the company to optimize your chances of successful implementation.

2. **Make sure your core competencies and strategies are aligned and can help fulfill your vision:** Core competencies are the core areas of your business that sets you apart from other businesses.

   These may be skills, tools, resources, or other things that allow you to be the best at what you do (ideally, all three of these things are aligned for truly unbeatable performance). We'll talk about this in detail in further sections.

   Make your strategies specific and achievable within a timeframe of no longer than twelve to twenty-four months.

   Once your initial strategies have been achieved, it will be time to create your next wave of strategies to build upon your new capabilities!

3. **Integrate throughout your organization.** Integrate *both* your vision *and* your strategies. Employees perform best when they know *what* they should be doing *and* why.

   Make sure that each department's sub-vision and strategy connects to the overarching strategies and vision of the company. Try to give each department a clear image of their role in the larger vision - as well as the roles of other departments.

4. **Translate those strategies into things you can clearly measure.** Your team is more likely to cross the finish line when all of your runners know exactly where it is, exactly what it looks like, and exactly what they need to do to get there.

5. **Educate employees on precisely how they, individually, can contribute to your company's vision each day. Reward them for meeting goals if possible or appropriate.**

   If possible, give each employee or job role specific goals to allow them to measure their own individual progress or contribution. This could be daily or weekly to-do lists, daily or weekly performance goals, practice skill tests they can take, access to their department's live reports, or something else.

Nothing motivates people like a concrete sense of accomplishment and recognition and appreciation of that accomplishment.

6. If you can give this to your people on a daily or weekly basis, it will supercharge their performance.

7. **Evaluate and communicate progress. Communicate, communicate, communicate!**

8. **Deliver.** Cross the finish line!

Now celebrate, recognize, evaluate - and do it all over again!

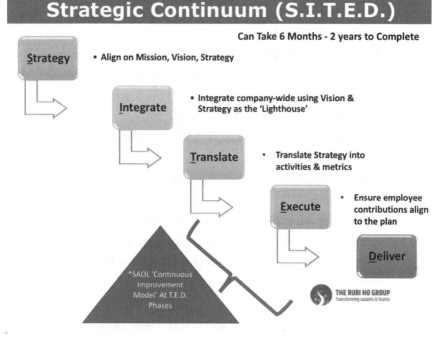

Created by Rubi Ho

At this point, some of you might be thinking: "But what does this 'mission and vision' stuff have to do with me? I'm not an executive or a department head. How can I reap the benefits of having mission and vision if my organizational leadership doesn't supply it?"

Well, easily.

The first step is to educate yourself on your organization's existing mission and vision. If that does not exist, or isn't functioning well, you can create your own mission and vision statement for yourself or your office group. Doing this will supercharge your performance and your job satisfaction.

When you know what your company cares about - or what *you* care about - you'll understand what it takes to *win* in it.

You'll be *much* more aware, engaged, and satisfied at work. You'll appear much *smarter* than your peers.

You'll make better decisions because of it, both for yourself *and* your company. You'll gain more from work and have a better experience while you're at it.

You'll be awake!

Chapter 6

Your Core Competencies

What are you good at?

There are many ways to think about this question. What did you go to school for? What sort of work are you most often praised for, or what sort of problem are you most often called upon to solve?

Where do things come *easily* for you? What subject areas and/or talents can you legitimately talk about for hours upon end?

Where are you most competent? What is your unique skillset? What sets you apart from others in terms of knowledge or capabilities?

> Core competencies are the traits, skills and/or primary capabilities that allow your company to *uniquely* live out your mission and vision.

In business, core competencies are the traits, skills and/or primary capabilities that allow your company to *uniquely* live out your mission and vision. Ideally, these set you apart from others. People do business with your business, or with you as an individual, because no one else can meet this particular need as well as you can.

These can be things that we studied or were trained in. They can be experiences and expertise we've acquired throughout our careers or personal lives. They can be innate talents or hobbies that have surprising applications in the business world.

To get a better idea of what core competencies look like and how they function, let's look at some examples of core competencies in different industries.

Let's start by looking at the New England Patriots. Like all NFL teams, the Patriots have core competencies in defense, offense, coaching staff and key trainers. All football teams *must* have a certain level of competency in all of these areas in order to function at the professional level.

I would argue however, that the Patriots have one unique core competency that other football teams in the league *don't* have, and that's their unique team system.

The Patriots' team system is known across the league and is now legendary because their framework allows their players to function better than traditional teams, *no matter who those players are.* The Patriots are able to plug almost *anyone* into their team system successfully and have generated six Super Bowl titles to prove it!

Their system, as noted in Sal Paolantonio's book, *How Football Explains America* consists of:

1. A militaristic, Navy-inspired approach due to Bill Belichick's close ties with the U.S. Naval Academy.
2. An emphasis on team well-being, and the importance of each player's role to the team.
3. Strong work ethic and preparation motivated by team success.
4. Versatile players who can play multiple positions if need be.
5. Multiple plans to take advantage of their competition's weaknesses, including backup plans and agility which allows the team to remain strategic even when the unexpected happens.[12]

The Patriots' unique core competency - its formula and expertise in creating winning teams - doesn't just meet the bare minimum standard an NFL team needs to meet. It has set them apart from the rest of the NFL, and they have become a dynasty that dominates the sport because of these unique skills and expertise.

Notice that this core competency would be easy to miss entirely

---

[12] Paolantonio S. *How Football Explains America*. Chicago, IL: Triumph Books; 2015.

if you operated according to traditional football assumptions. The Patriots' unique strength is not their offense, or their defense, or specific team positions or athletic skills.

Instead, the core competency that sets them apart is *their skill at team-building* - something you might miss entirely if you focused only on the results achieved by individual players, or their performance at athletic metrics.

If you didn't ask the right questions, you might think the Patriots were merely lucky to consistently receive the best players, or that their early success had created a self-sustaining loop that attracted the most successful players to the team that was already the most successful. You might never notice the true key to the Patriots' success if you didn't track player's performance both before and after joining the team.

For an example of unique core competencies in an individual, let's take myself. As a strategic and organizational leadership coach and consultant, I have core competencies in:

- **Strategy:** Gained from years of partnering with executives and teams to formulate success strategies across dozens of different industries over the course of decades.
- **Organizational Health:** Gained from both my formal education in organizational management *and* my hands-on experience optimizing a dizzying variety of organizations throughout the years.
- **Leadership and Enterprise Executive Coach:** Gained from both my formal education in executive coaching, and the hands-on experience of being part of an executive coaching firm, having been an adjunct professor in executive coaching in multiple universities, and working with hundreds of individuals and their teams on improving their leadership skills.
- **Performance Management:** Gained from my formal education in performance management and my background in curriculum and program design, as well as countless hours

spent helping individuals and teams improve their overall business and leadership performance.

In my life - as is probably also true in yours - you see core competencies that arise as a combination of formal education with hands-on experience. In my case, I even have unique personal background which required me to make very efficient use of very scarce resources and to learn to think outside the box when solving problems.

When combined, my core competencies help separate me from others in my field. I not only coach - I also consult with entire organizations. I don't only consult, but I also coach individual executives and workers.

I'm a true business and leadership partner for organizations. I can help them grow at both the systemic and individual levels. I am able to tackle almost *any* problem at the company, team and individual level because of my unique set of core competencies.

What are your most unique core competencies? What are you better at than anybody else because of your personal background, personal and professional experiences, formal education, and upbringing?

> ..it's often the things that *aren't* taught in schools - making them less accessible to the competition - which set one business or team apart from others in performance.

Don't restrict yourself to just formal degrees and class titles when asking this question. If you do, you may miss some very important life skills that others who do not come from a background like your own may not have had the opportunity to learn in formal degree programs.

Formal education competencies are very important, as colleges and business schools try to teach the most vital and commonly required skills to their students. But it's often the things that *aren't* taught in schools - making them less accessible to the competition - which set one business or team apart from others in performance.

Last but not least, let's look at a corporate example of unique core competencies. In particular, let's take Amazon and look at their current vision statement:

"To be Earth's most customer-centric company; to build a place where people can come to find and discover anything they might want to buy-online."

In my opinion, Amazon's core competencies revolve around the following abilities:

1. **Distribution:** As of late Feb 2019, Amazon has gone through massive efforts to own the end to end distribution process. They had over 200 million square feet of fulfillment space, sorting centers, delivery stations, Prime hubs and even Prime air hubs![13]

2. **Digital Footprint/Shelf Space:** Remember, almost 38% of all US online purchases are Amazon purchases! They've accomplished this through a combination of high availability and almost endless inventory.

    Amazon's extensive digital "shelf space" meant that there was almost nothing customers would have to leave the website in order to buy, making it the most comprehensive and convenient one-stop shop for most customers.

3. **Pricing:** Because of Amazon's huge digital footprint, they are able to hold digital shelf space and therefore control pricing. Because most companies know that half of *all* online sales depend on being listed on Amazon, companies are generally willing to list their products on Amazon at competitive low prices.

4. **Product Diversity:** Coupled with their market share and digital shelf space, who *doesn't* shop on Amazon? For many shoppers, it's the go-to destination if you aren't certain how or where to find a product.

---

[13] https://www.theatlantic.com/technology/archive/2019/02/when-amazon-went-from-big-to-unbelievably-big/582097/

Amazon's core competencies have allowed them to become the Walmart of the digital, online, e-commerce space in the United States. They are widely viewed as *the* place to find almost anything, and to find it at affordable prices.

Amazon has accomplished all of this by emphasizing a few basic core competencies:

- The ability to run an online marketplace efficiently,
- The ability to physically handle huge volume and variety of products quickly and efficiently, and
- The ability to create a highly competitive environment that keeps consumer prices down.

I hope you understand what core competencies are *and* how important they are to fulfilling your vision.

Your core competencies are the engine that drives you to your vision. They are what allows you to stay in business, by having consumers choose to give you their money instead of giving it to someone else.

Knowing what your core competencies are is *very* important, whether you apply them to yourself as an individual, or at the company level.

In fact, it could be argued that your core competencies are even *more* important than your vision. In many ways, your vision is a means to the end of nurturing and leveraging your core competencies. A properly constructed vision is one that ensures your core competencies are being used to full advantage, and that necessary core competencies for your mission are being constantly maintained and developed.

So if you find yourself having mission, vision, or virtually any other type of business obstacle, take a moment to re-examine your core competencies.

Are you putting the most resources into the areas where your skills are strongest - in other words, the areas that yield the strongest return on investment?

Or are your strategies, products, and plans neglecting your strongest skills and pouring effort into tasks that aren't what you're best at?

Asking a few important questions will help you make sure that your core competencies continue to serve you by getting great ROI and producing happy customers.

Are Your Core Competencies Still Marketable?

If not, never fear - if you act quickly in pursuit of your mission, your core competencies can be updated and replaced.

Remember Kodak? One of their biggest core competencies was paper photography. In the 20th century, they were known for producing paper and chemical solutions which gave consumers access to paper photography more quickly and beautifully than anyone else.[14]

But let me ask you: when was the last time you held a paper photo in your hand that wasn't printed from a digital file? When was the last time someone you knew took a Polaroid picture - one that developed instantly from film to photo paper instead of being saved digitally for instant and permanent sharing?

It's not hard to see why Kodak suffered: its core competency became largely unmarketable as digital media became superior to paper media for most consumers' purposes.

Could Kodak somehow have seen the end coming and replace their primary core competency because it was no longer relevant? Could they have become frontrunners in the field of digital photography by watching the photography market closely and seamlessly transitioning their customers from paper to digital photography solutions?

> **Accomplishing agility requires conscious forethought and planning, since a company's natural impulse is to become comfortable with current market conditions and assume they will not change.**

Could Kodak have used their photography expertise to develop the best digital photography systems out there at a time when digital pioneers were focusing on other applications of their technologies?

Why didn't Kodak change fast or drastically enough?

The answer for many companies is simply that their leadership

---

[14] https://www.forbes.com/sites/chunkamui/2012/01/18/how-kodak-failed/ #1540a32c6f27

and organizations are not agile enough. They don't see and respond to changes fast enough in the executive suite - or they see the changing necessities but can't muster the physical or personnel resources to actually implement the change in their business model before it's too late.

We'll discuss strategies to avoid Kodak's pitfall and ensure your company's agility in a changing market later in this book.

For now, remember this keyword: agility.

Agility is the ability of a company or team to respond to changing conditions. Accomplishing agility requires conscious forethought and planning, since a company's natural impulse is to become comfortable with current market conditions and assume they will not change.

Having agility is key to almost every modern successful company or individual. It's also necessary for our next core competency cultivation principle.

Are You Fully Leveraging Your Core Competencies?

Look at what you're best at, as a company or an individual. Are you using this core competency every day?

Are you offering it to your customers each and every day - at the premium price that a unique core competency deserves? Are these strongest skills receiving most of your company's investment of resources, resulting in the highest possible ROI for those investments?

If the answer to any of those questions is "no," you might be experiencing some common organizational problems. You might be feeling like daily operations is an uphill battle, or like you're throwing money into operations that just aren't yielding return.

If you trace this problem to its root, you'll likely find that you're depending on, and investing in, tasks and skills that simply are not your company's strongest core competencies.

If your core competencies are *not* being leveraged fully, you need to re-strategize. You'll find that doing so can increase efficiency, ease, and profit margins.

If your core competencies are the engine to fulfilling your vision, they need to be healthy and fully leveraged. Imagine having a 400 HP power car and only using first gear - then getting frustrated because you're not moving fast enough!

Evaluate Your Core Competencies Regularly

For optimal performance, it's useful to take a quarterly or annual evaluation of your individual and organizational core competencies. Ask yourself:

- What are we better at than anyone else? Include skills, hands-on experience, physical equipment and capabilities, market share and reputation.
- Out of the things we do, what are we best at? What comes most easily to us, is the highest-quality work, or produces the highest return on investment?
- Of the things we do, what is *most* in-demand on the market right now? Is there anything we do that is beginning to be replaced by a new competitor, or are there any emerging technologies or market niches that we could be using our core competencies to dominate?

Once you've got a list of your three to twelve core competencies, make and honest and objective assessment of each. Give it an overall grade, determine what you need to do to:

- Improve and maintain your core competencies' performance under current and future market conditions.
- Ensure that your core competency is being offered to customers in the most efficient and profitable possible ways.
- Develop new supporting core competencies to allow you to continue leveraging your most important skills and equipment.

Below are the core competencies of a healthcare corporation I worked with in years past. After helping them re-solidify their mission, purpose and vision, they listed their core competencies as follows:

Our Mission
We provide choices for people to live independently in the place they want to call home.
What We Specifically Provide
• We provide advocacy, assistance and answers to the aging and those with disabilities. • We provide long-term care in the home and/or community.
Our Vision
We will be the premiere health corporation in the tri-state area by offering best-in-class case management and senior citizen and disability advocacy.

Created by Rubi Ho

Our Core Competencies

Care Management	Eligibility, evaluation and assessment of needs by experts.
Resource coordination and allocation	Provider management and development.
Care transition expertise.	Advocacy, education and awareness of senior citizens.

Created by Rubi Ho

Key Benefits of Your Core Competencies

It's important to be conscious of how core competencies can benefit you if you want to reap those benefits!

It's hard to optimize something you're not aware of, or consciously prioritizing. So let's review the benefits of your core competencies:

- Your core competencies are the primary vehicle that will allow you to bring your vision to fulfillment.
- Your core competencies show the most efficient way for you to derive income and make money.
- The unique combination of your core competencies and the value they provide gives you an edge over your competitors in the marketplace.
- Your core competencies allow you to provide excellent, unparalleled service, further building your company brand.

Year after year, it's on you to continually live out your mission, fulfill your vision, formulate new goals, and ensure that your core competencies remain healthy and market-relevant. No one is going to do it for you!

Remember: You Are Your Own CEO

We've spoken a lot in this chapter about matters that might seem specific to organizations and corporations. After all, individuals are less likely to have unique equipment, distribution networks, and whole fleets of experts.

But *everything* we've said here applies to individuals just as much as it does to businesses.

What are your core competencies? Are you leveraging them fully when you strategize about the best ways to reach your goals?

Could you be more profitable or more powerful if you leveraged them more? Are you overlooking a massive asset you have because it's not a formal degree or training certificate?

Remember, you're taking advice from someone who once was a Vietnamese refugee, an orphan, and a street punk, who is now involved in helping the leaders of $90 billion companies with leadership, strategy and organizational health!

Nothing I say is ever intended *only* for corporations. In fact, nothing in life is!

All of the same skills and formulas that make a corporation highly successful will make an individual highly successful as well.

It's so crazy how far I've come as an individual. That experience of personal growth is what allows me to give priceless growth advice to everyone from Fortune 500 CEOs to street punks like my younger self.

If *I* can do it, there's no doubt in my mind that *you* can do it too!

Just have faith in yourself. And maybe have some faith in the words of a street punk who's just a little more experienced than you in business and in life.

Let's move on to strategy. Whether for an individual pursuit or a business model, this is the game plan which tells you exactly how to use your core competencies to achieve your mission and vision.

Chapter 7

Your Strategy

We talk about strategy constantly in our American culture. We play strategy-based games to try to beat each other at them. We discuss having strategies for meeting any and every goal we might have. To date, a Google search on strategy generates over 600 million results![15]

The word "strategy" is a noun that means:

a. A plan of action to achieve a major or overall aim
b. The *art* of planning and directing a military operation during a war or battle

Let's get a little more specific. After all, simply saying it's "a plan" doesn't tell us what kind of strategy is the best, what a great strategy must have, or how to make one. And there are crucial differences between very good strategies and strategies that are almost useless.

So instead let's start with *my personal* definition of strategy which is:

"A plan to achieve a goal or overall aim by making the most efficient use of resources possible, **and** *with the ability to change plans if necessary, especially if external conditions change for the worse."*

Hopefully, you are already thinking that your strategy needs to

---

[15] https://www.google.com/search/strategy

make intelligent use of your core competencies, heavily leveraging what you do best in an efficiency and an optimized cost mindset.

You might also recognize that it needs to have built-in agility and include built-in checkpoints to re-evaluate your vision and core competencies as a safeguard against any unforeseen development which might threaten your goals.

Creating a strategy for yourself or your organization is a lot like predicting the path of a hurricane. You are doing your best to be right *most* of the time, but know you will often miss the mark due to some unexpected 'changes in the wind.'

For that reason, strategy must be able to respond organically to changing conditions, with an agile and continuous improvement mindset. The likelihood that you will have to pivot and change course at some point in your life and career journey, or even your fiscal year, is high.

There are many experts and great books on strategy. One of my all-time favorites is "Scaling Up" by Verne Harnish.[16] It's a great best practices book for *everything* regarding organizational strategy and covers specific best practices more thoroughly than I'll have time to do here. I highly recommend you give it a read if you are, or someday hope to be, working in a decision-making capacity for any sort of organization.

My own strategic approach is derived from a combination of street smarts, my competitive nature, formal education, and my real life experience of seeing what works and what doesn't while having to make the most of very scarce resources.

I begin by defining strategy in very specific terms, which act as a checklist for creating a great strategy without fail.

> **Nothing about strategy is done in a vacuum. *All* actions you take and decisions you make have both external and internal impact. Being *strategic* and applying *strategy* in an optimal way means taking every interaction into account, lest one of them derail your plan.**

---

[16] Harnish V. *Scaling Up*. How few companies make it and why the rest don't. Ashburn, VA: Gazelles Inc; 2014.

Now let's get into the weeds a little and refine strategy even more by saying it is:

"The actions and priorities you take to fulfill your mission, vision and/or goals *after* taking into account your:

- ❑ Core Competencies
- ❑ Environment
- ❑ Financials
- ❑ People
- ❑ Processes
- ❑ Leadership
- ❑ Infrastructure
- ❑ Capability
- ❑ Sense of Urgency

I challenge you to take a moment right now, on your own or with your team to move down the checklist I provided and write down all of your important findings, questions, and answers on each bullet point on that list.

You'll soon find yourself considering questions, assets, and potential obstacles you'd otherwise have missed.

Has somebody heard about a potential change in the market that you might want to pay attention to or need to address? Is your team optimally structured and ready to be fully leveraged and perform? Do your teammates share the same sense of urgency about what goals need to be achieved and what steps need to be taken to achieve them?

Nothing about strategy is done in a vacuum. *All* actions you take and decisions you make have both external and internal impact. Being *strategic* and applying *strategy* in an optimal way means taking every interaction into account, lest one of them derail your plan. It means:

- *Not* making decisions based on the view of isolated, non-communicating silos within your organization.

You must ensure that you have all the information about your organization's big picture and internal workings, and have taken into account how your actions will affect other team members.

- Being empathetic to others' needs as well as your own.

Remember, taking into account human needs isn't "a necessary evil." It's part of the essential care and keeping of your assets, just as much as caring for and maintaining your equipment or your financials.

- Ensuring your actions complement and *don't* contradict the vision. Remember, this may require stepping out of your own silo and taking into account the viewpoints of other players on your team!
- Being cognizant of the actual 'spend' and budget you *know* you have - not the budget you wish you had or hope to have.
- Incorporating past experiences, mistakes and lessons into your decisions.

Has something gone wrong in the past? Then you must have a plan for what to do if it goes wrong again. Has a goal failed to be achieved in the past? Then you must analyze *why* and incorporate a fix into later strategies.

There are two types of "buckets" of strategy. I separate them according to time frame in an attempt to ensure that we maintain both short-term and long-term thinking:

- Short term, within 18-24 months and
- Long term, greater than 24 months .

Most acute problem-solving occurs in the short-term. I typically get called in as a resolver when an organization is experiencing some type of down-turn or situation and they need an immediate fix, fast.

The reason for this might be obvious: it's easier to pivot a long-term strategy, because problems that are expected to manifest more than 24 months out are less acute and less urgent.

But it's also obvious that long-term success *depends* on short-term success. You're not going to meet your three-year goal if you're consistently missing your quarterly goals and you don't know how to fix this.

Whether short-term or long-term, the path towards building out your strategy is the same. The same questions must be asked and answered for optimal results.

The sense of urgency however, is a whole lot higher to 'get it right' if you have an immediate problem that needs quick resolution. That's why senior leaders need to empower and arm their captains - be those executive officers, departmental directors, or personnel managers - to make bold, informed, and effective decisions to right the ship in an efficient and reliable way.

Building an Unbeatable Strategy

There's a reason we've discussed mission, vision, and core competencies *before* strategy. All of these things are important *because* they are indispensable as strategic prerequisites.

You wouldn't set out on a strategic military mission for example, without a known destination or goal (mission), a map to follow to get there (vision), and the set of tools and skills you need to get the job done (core competencies).

In just the same way, if you set out without a clear destination, a road map, and a set of tools and skills you've chosen with this specific mission in mind, you're unlikely to achieve your goals in the highly competitive world of business.

So how do we make our mission, vision, and core competencies work together as reliably and efficiently as possible? To do this, we must formulate key *Strategic Initiatives* that will help fulfill our vision or follow our road map to success.

Remember, the formulation of our strategic initiatives takes place only after we have taken a complete look at both our internal and external variables mentioned previously.

If you haven't gone down that bulleted list and asked and answered questions about each and every point on it, I strongly urge you to do so before you continue. Only then will you be fully prepared to practice my optimal strategy for making strategy!

Whether you conduct a SWOT (Strengths, Weaknesses, Opportunities, Threats) analysis, look at Porter's 5 Forces, use the best practices contained in "Scaling Up," hire a consultant, or use another tool or strategy to do your gap-analysis doesn't matter.

What's important is that you are doing a 'whole picture' analysis before coming up with your initiatives. You're thinking ahead and asking the right questions - and thereby minimizing the chances that you'll look back a year from now and say "I wish I'd thought of that back then."

Case Study

Remember that healthcare organization whose core competencies we saw earlier? Let's see how they leveraged those to create and implement a strategy for success.

Here's the key analysis of the self-evaluation they completed using the checklist above, prior to formulating their strategies.

Notice the points where this analysis directly translated into the creation of strategic goals to leverage core competencies or counter potential threats:

- ỹ *Core Competencies:* The company's competencies were strong on the expertise side but weak on the leveraging side. They needed to grow their ability to offer consumers more concrete benefits using their tremendous expertise.
- ỹ *Environment:* There was an opportunity to grow into new markets, but they had to act swiftly or other new entrants would take hold. Externally, their company brand was weak and skewed towards only a few of their strengths. This impaired their ability to take advantage of opportunities.
- ỹ *Financials:* The company was profitable, but funding was expected to dwindle from the government sector within two years. This was projected to have a drastic financial impact of at least 20% to their bottom line.
- ỹ *People:* Turnover was not high, but employees were complacent and confused about their mission and vision as there was no clarity or unified voice among leadership. This led to lower performance and resistance to proactive change.
- ỹ *Processes:* The organization lacked a process to grow and seize new markets. At the beginning of our strategy session, they viewed their consumers as a limited pool and did not see any way they could expand their reach or consumer base.
- ỹ *Leadership:* Leadership was initially *not* aligned on what to focus on for the next 18-24 months. There was disagreement based on specialization, as often occurs when organizational

duties are heavily siloed with little communication between departments or specialties.

ŷ *Infrastructure:* Infrastructure was a combination of both manual and automated processes. Strengths and weaknesses in that area were crucial to determining the company's abilities as a healthcare provider, but had not been analyzed or evaluated critically for some time.

ŷ *Capability:* Resources were limited, especially from the funding and IT channels. Before the conscious strategic analysis, IT was simply ignored and discounted, subconsciously viewed by other departments as a mere nuisance or insurmountable obstacle rather than an ally or asset.

ŷ *Sense of Urgency:* The window of growth opportunity had to be seized within the next 18-24 months to ward off new competitors who could be expected to attempt to enter the market in that time.

Based on their biggest 'pain points' and areas of opportunity, the organization prioritized 4 key strategic initiatives to tackle. Their immediate next step was then to build out the 'master game-plan'/ roadmap with concrete steps that would be used to roll it out within their organization.

Primary Strategic Focus Areas for 18-24 Months
1. Fully leverage and communicate our Brand and Unique Business Model, inclusive of our Core Competencies throughout the external health community
2. A. Maximize our Procurement Partnerships B. Maintain our staple programs
3. Grow new markets by 20%, with target growth rate of 10% per year
4. Achieve a unified, consolidated, and collective state-wide 'voice' and message among our partnership network

Created by Rubi Ho

*"Rubi worked with our association of leaders from across the state.**In seven hours** he brought people together to define their common mission and goals. We identified the core competencies and next steps for us as an association which will help set us up for success for years to come.-CEO"*

This shows the power of mission, vision, core competency evaluation, and ultimately strategy to transform a business' prospects and its future.

Chapter 8

A Closer Look at The Strategic *Variables*

In this chapter we'll take a deeper dive into each of the strategic variables to help you understand their power more fully. The point here is to be thorough in your understanding.

The more thoroughly you understand these concepts and how they play together, the more effectively you'll be able to avoid roadblocks and create clearer, more on point strategies.

You'll be able to better leverage the resources you have. You'll be able to better anticipate and prepare for threats. You might even find hidden strengths within your organization that you didn't know existed.

Core Competencies

Remember, Core Competencies are the key 'unique value' components of your company. I've often seen situations where simply assessing how well *each* Core Competency is performing is sufficient to determine your strategies for the next 18-24 months.

This idea of assessing exactly how well you perform different tasks may seem simple, but it is often shockingly neglected - at great cost - by organizations who assume they know what their core competencies *should* be or how well these *must* be functioning.

Some tips to avoid being in the dark about your most important assets and values include:

1. Give each Core Competency an evaluation regularly, rating each on a 10 point or 5 point scale.

If possible, have each member of your leadership team or each departmental director perform this rating independently to see where any weaknesses or unrealized strengths may be hiding.

2. Get the entire leadership team together and talk through your rationale for your assessments. Is someone seeing an unleveraged strength or hidden problem that the rest of the team is missing?

3. Determine your priorities.

   Which underutilized strengths could be used to offer drastically more value to the company or reduce operating costs? Which hidden weaknesses might be driving loss of market share or difficulty in acquiring new customers?

4. Start to initialize solutions and see where you can leverage the under-utilized areas and start repairing the broken ones.

Let's look at how one company I worked with evaluated, leveraged, and developed core competencies.

Revenues were drastically down for the Sales Distribution department of one company I worked with. This was a huge problem because Sales Distribution was considered one of their key Core Competencies - in other words, it was *supposed* to be one of their few major drivers of value.

We spent an entire year focusing on strategies that looked at new markets, growing our market share with current clients, maximizing our profit margin and optimizing our Opex (Operational expenses) for the next year.

Our in-depth analysis found both underutilized strengths, and under-addressed weaknesses that had arisen as a result of market changes over time.

The results of this strategic analysis? Within 6 months, the organization went from being below target with negative margins to increasing profit margin by 3% or a positive 2 million dollars.

Three percent might sound like modest growth, but when you initially start the year negative, those results can mean the difference between an organization's long-term triumph and its dissolution.

The Environment

The environment is where a SWOT (Strengths, Weaknesses, Opportunities, Threats) analysis or Porter's Five Forces Model (see below)[17] can really help you take a "wholistic look at your situation. Success, after all, is determined by *both* your internal company's strengths and weaknesses, *and* the external environment. Environmental factors may include competition, suppliers, vendors, new technologies, new or dwindling markets, etc..

You might have noticed something that several of our spectacular business failures from early in this book had in common. Toys 'R' Us, K-Mart, Sears, and other once-great companies disappeared rapidly *because they didn't take into account changes to the external environment.* They failed to adjust to the rise of the Internet, which made physical "big box" stores actually less useful to consumers than online retailers in many cases.

Failure to take your external environment into account means you're operating in a bubble. Your consumers are left out in the cold - which becomes a problem for *you* very quickly when other companies become more responsive and appealing to their needs.

As I write this book, the US is in the midst of a tariff 'battle' with China; over 50% of shale companies are on the road to bankruptcy due to declining oil barrel prices; Ford is re-investing in manufacturing jobs; hurricane Dorian (Category 5) is spinning out of control in the Atlantic; Venezuela is selling off its gold for Euros to stay alive; there is talk of an impending recession; and it is an election year.

Any one of those recent developments could make or break your company, depending on what industry and geographic location you're in.

Any one of them could present a marvelous opportunity for growth into a new sector - or a lethal threat that needs to be handled swiftly and decisively before it can kill.

And that's just a one-paragraph look at the world around us!

---

[17] https://www.investopedia.com/terms/p/porter.asp

An extensive environmental analysis - preferably more thorough than the one I just did here - is *critical* to avoiding disaster *and* making the most of opportunities for growth.

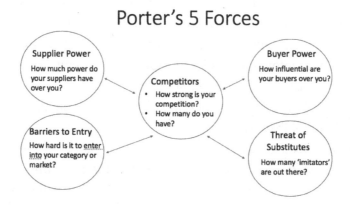

Porter's 5 Forces Chart created by Rubi Ho

The Financials

Financials! Financials! Financials!

Companies live or die for *one* reason: they have cash, or they don't!

Cash is to companies what food is to an animal; you'll do just about anything to get it, because if you don't, you'll die.

Don't run out of cash!

This means you have to be careful with your cash. Did you know that the brains of animals are designed to

***Don't* run out of cash!**

conserve calories and avoid "wasting" energy on pursuits that don't help them survive? A company must behave exactly the same way; if you are spending cash on something that isn't helping you get more cash, you may die.

The flow of cash is also seen to be commensurate to the line of credit that a company has. An organization's overall health and odds of survival are dependent on its financial health and income. This means that good financial performance must be incentivized at every level of the company, just as each organ of the body knows that it will die if an animal starves.

If a budget is in place and you go over budget, the department that is responsible for that budget should be the department that sees the cuts.

If that means a plan is scrapped, then scrap it. The person that put the budget in place needs to be held accountable by the CEO and BOD (Board of Directors) over what happened and formally reprimanded or released.

As we mentioned earlier, accountability doesn't *just* mean immediately jumping to blame scapegoats. Questions should also be asked to determine and confirm the root cause of the failure.

Blaming an individual or department for failing might be worse than useless if the accountability actually rests higher up - perhaps with a systemic policy or decision-maker who did not give the department the resources it needed to succeed.

If a bad policy is starving departments, your localized failures may be the canaries in the coal mine, and blaming them may lead to bigger problems down the road.

But *someone* needs to be held accountable for failures to stick to budget. This may mean reprimanding or releasing an individual, reprimanding or releasing their boss, or changing a company-wide policy or resources.

And remember, the person or policy who's held accountable needs to be something *within the company's ability to control*. Blaming forces beyond your control is also worse than useless because it does nothing to solve the problem or improve future outcomes.

It's all about accountability. Finding where accountability for success and failure rests is one of the strongest skills a leader can have.

This is the skill of finding hidden strengths and weaknesses - and ultimately building the strongest organization possible as a result.

One of my dear friends, a dynamo CEO shared his wisdom with me around financials:

"Rubi, if you want to successfully run any company, you must be able to always follow the money. It will tell you where you are winning. It will tell you where you are losing. My mentor told me this when I was in my late 20's. I've been a successful CEO now for over 25 years now. It hasn't failed me yet!"

Although I understood the concept of *not* running out of cash, I did not always appreciate the importance of money and financials as I do now. The difference today is experience.

I've worked with many organizations in various structures, markets, and industries. As a result, I now have a *much* better understanding of how cash and finances as a whole:

- o   Keep the lights on
- o   Pay the wages
- o   Pay the Opex (Operating expenses)

- ○ Enable Acquisitions
- ○ Pay stockholders and/or owners
- ○ Enable savings
- ○ Enable collateral
- ○ Enable leverage
- ○ Pay for commissions and bonuses
- ○ Impact the wider market
- ○ Determine the actual value of your company
- ○ Determine whether to, invest, hire more staff, and buy more assets

Need I go on?

Knowing where you stand financially in itself is a matter of strategic competence. Finances will serve as one of your *primary* go/ no go 'stop-gates' to what strategies you can or can't take.

Ultimately, there is only so much leveraging risk you can afford to take. Sometimes, you simply *can't* take on anymore financial risk at all because *one* more failure and your company will be sunk!

Some of you may be thinking that this is incredibly obvious. "Of *course* organizations need money to function, Rubi. Everyone knows that."

Yet many organizations *don't* take basic and vital steps to help them survive financially. For example, it is *critical* to have a financial expert on your team!

I'm not talking about a bookkeeper or accountant. No disrespect to the great accountants who keep the world turning, but they are typically not specialized in financial expertise such as investments, markets, and growth strategies.

I'm talking about a financial *strategist*. Someone who is both *very* competent financially *and* is able to think like a CEO and strategically as well.

Such experts are often seen as "unnecessary" by executives, business owners, or even individuals who assume they know "enough" about financial markets to get by. But how often do these self-proclaimed experts miss out on major windfalls or take major losses because of some lack of expert knowledge?

Find a great financial specialist and he or she will become one of your *primary* business partners for life. This is true whether you're an individual, a small business, or a Fortune 500 CEO!

The importance of finances to strategy alone deserves a book's worth of discussion. There are literally hundreds of thousands of books on finances, and for good reason.

Having spent over a decade working with corporate leaders and entrepreneurs alike, I find that financial acumen is an area where ambitious people are often severely lacking.

The good news for you is, that means there's an easy way to give yourself a competitive edge. Do some research to determine the best way for you to gain financial acumen, or add a financial expert to your team, today.

Know Your Numbers

I hate to blame society and education - things we can't control as individuals or business leaders - for our trouble with numbers. But in this case, it has to be said. The way we think about numbers is far from optimal, and it's because of the way we are taught.

We learn almost *nothing* in school about how to handle money *or* make money. We are often taught that that's someone else's job to worry about, and that our job is simply to accept the wages we are given. This does not prepare *anybody* to be executives or to make decisions about handling and making money.

What a shame! This is one of the primary reasons why so many people in our society are in debt, even including our own government.

Practice managing and making your money. Whether you're a CEO, a business owner, or an individual, think about how to minimize costs while maximizing your well-being.

Money isn't infinite, after all. And that's the secret of it. Money is power and you can only make money by *having* money in the first place. At least in business, those who can turn a small amount of money into a large amount are the most powerful people in our society.

You don't have to be a financial expert, but you *should* know enough about your company's numbers to know if someone is "blowing smoke up your ass" when they're talking about them!

That's the reason I finally bit the bullet and got my executive MBA after spending years working in business without that formal education. Before that point, I "kind of" understood what all the numbers meant, but not enough to make *any* kind of strategic decisions around them.

Now, I've not only lost my feeling of intimidation around numbers - I never make *any* strategic decisions without checking all the important numbers first.

A CEO's *primary* responsibility is to 'make money' for the company. But even if you're not the CEO of the company you work for, you can help her out by being a good steward of financial operations within your own department or job description.

Numbers and finances are two of the most crucial components of being an effective business leader. But just as important to your strategy are the people on your team.

These are the most important moving parts of your business. That's why it's vital to account for...

People and Strategic Leadership

Do you have "the right people on the bus?" Does your team have the talent, competency, capability, and drive they need to execute your strategies successfully?

We'll talk about your people *much* more when we take a deep dive into leadership in a later chapter. But right now, it's important to emphasize that without the right team in place, your strategies might as well be pipe dreams.

Successful strategic execution requires not only the correct skills to get the job done, but also the necessary drive and agility from your team.

This is why mission and vision are such crucial motivating factors: with a compelling mission and vision to motivate them, your team can move mountains. But without a clear understanding of why you're proposing changes or what you're trying to accomplish, your team may encounter resistance, confusion, or apathy.

At the minimum, the leader/owner of your strategy *must* have skills and drives that complement the strategy itself.

Any given strategy will fall into one of the following categories:

Disruptive. Innovative, and Growth Strategies

Strategies that 'shake things up' and cause growth are often necessary to create radical transformations within a company, in order to adapt to changing technology and market conditions. **This type of strategy will require that the leader is *also* disruptive in nature.**

You don't want a dictator or someone with no people skills, but he or she has to have the direct, "take no prisoners," decisive and transformational ability to take other employees far outside of their comfort zones.

This leader must have both the passion and the confidence to lead the company to the promised land. This is a leader who's willing to take risks and manage those risks.

If you try to hand a disruptive strategy to a leader who is timid, quiet, or very attached and invested in the old way of doing things, you'll find yourself facing an execution failure.

Optimization Strategies

This strategy does not require radical changes, but does require many small changes to improve company operations wherever possible. This requires an attitude of perpetual commitment to 'make things better than they are today.'

The ideal leader in this scenario is one who is extremely competent in things like lean, six sigma, supply chain, and operations.

She still has to have strong leadership skills but attention to detail is more important in this role than big-picture vision. In fact, someone who prefers to implement big, radical ideas may have difficulty focusing her attention on small or "boring" but vital process changes.

Maintenance Strategies

This is where you will be required to continue doing what you're doing *while maintaining the same level of excellence.*

In this scenario, the leader is responsible for maintaining everything that's working. Usually, it's because the company is hitting all its marks, financially and in other performance areas.

This type of strategy is excellent for a leader who is invested in keeping order and maintaining the way things are being done already. The leader who might be precisely wrong to implement a disruptive strategy might be just the man you need to implement a maintenance strategy.

Make Sure You Have The Right Strategy-Leader Match

I've seen countless situations where the strategy was right on-target - on paper, that is - but the company had the wrong leader "match" for the strategy. The result was mysterious failure to meet strategy goals, and recurring doubts and frustrations.

There was nothing wrong with the strategy - it was just that the thought process, attitude, or social skills of the leader in place were not a good match to implement it.

After all, people aren't machines. Personality and worldview are just as big a part of our core competencies as our degrees or work experience and it's just as important to leverage these by placing them intelligently as it is to have the right mechanical equipment or formal certifications for the job.

Once you understand the above differences in strategy types, you'll clearly know if you have the right leader in place, or if perhaps it's time to deputize a new strategy champion.

We've mentioned here how your people and their core competencies are at least as important as your physical equipment. But when creating a strategy, it *is* vitally important to do it with consideration for your physical resources and processes. This includes your digital platforms.

So when strategizing, be sure to evaluate your...

Infrastructure and Processes

Process is a vital aspect of strategy that ensures consistent quality of work. Your process determines the financial cost of getting your work done as efficiently and optimally as possible, and in a sustainable way.

Some companies meticulously optimize and document their processes for completing specific tasks to ensure that things are being done the same way - and the best way - every time. Others don't.

Everything worth doing well warrants a process. When you discover a process or formula that works well, you want to ensure that it is written down, documented, taught, and then followed consistently throughout your organization.

In that way, you can ensure that the ideas of the most innovative and efficient people in your company are transformed into a process that any employee can follow and repeat. This drastically increases the efficiency of your whole organization.

Processes can be used to maximize your company's efficiency, both by leveraging the ideas of your most innovative people *and* by leveraging empirical and analytical research.

Entire professions exist of employees and consultants who conduct research to scientifically discover ways to optimize a company's process so as to save minutes, dollars, or materials - every time an action is repeated anywhere within the organization.

In fact, without good process documentation and training in place, companies are not able to grow or scale up. Being able to scale up means you are able to repeat what you are doing and you are able to rapidly and reliably teach new workers to do it effectively.

From the strategic perspective, this is a critical area that must be addressed and not glossed over. Your personnel are only as good as your processes. No matter how innately talented they are, they are unlikely to independently stumble across the best possible way to do things many times over.

You might want to grow your business by 20% next year, but are your processes in place for you to be able to do this? Do you know exactly which processes work best for approaching new potential clients, and which don't? Do you have the procedures, documentation, and training program to increase your staff as needed to accommodate the increased workload?

In IT, are your hardware and software platforms able to handle the increased data flow and management? In manufacturing and shipping, do you have the machines, materials, storage space, and transportation capabilities to be able to handle the demand that your financial targets require?

In operations, are the processes automated, or are they manual? If they are manual, who is training new workers, and are the materials they are using optimized and updated?

Across the company, do your processes "speak to one another," or are they siloed without the ability to respond to changing realities in other departments?

Do you even have process documentation? Or are you just hoping that new team members will "figure it out" as they go along?

Do the processes need to be audited by a third party to justify their worth? Are your processes already performing to your standards, or might it be worth consulting an

> **Those who don't break through and learn to train others to perform just as well as they perform themselves remain single-person entrepreneurs for the rest of their lives instead of going on to found large companies.**

independent expert to see if they can be improved, potentially saving millions of dollars or thousands of staff hours per year?

Get the picture?

Sometimes, once we realize our processes are *not* scalable in their current forms, creating scalable processes becomes a primary strategic goal. For some organizations, in fact, the ability to create and teach effective processes becomes *the* growth-limiting factor for the organization.

In fact, this is one of the primary struggle areas for entrepreneurs who'd like to grow their businesses. Entrepreneurs often start off as a "one person show," where a lone entrepreneur is doing performing all the business functions and wearing all the hats.

As a result, new entrepreneurs often end up with no process for effectively teaching new team members, and are unable to grow their business' revenue past their own personal performance limits as a result. Breaking through the "one person show" dilemma becomes the ceiling for growth of an otherwise extremely promising business.

Having scalable processes, in this case, is the only possible "ceiling breaker." Those who don't break through and learn to train others to perform just as well as they perform themselves remain single-person entrepreneurs for the rest of their lives instead of going on to found large companies.

As long as it's an intentional choice, being a one-person entrepreneur is not necessarily a bad thing. It may align with a person's personality or goals.

But it *should* be just that: a choice that is freely made because it's the entrepreneur's favorite option. Too many brilliant entrepreneurs remain as one-person operations, not because this is their wildest dream, but simply because they do not take the time to develop and implement scalable processes.

Here's a personal example from my own life of the importance of process to any business that wishes to grow.

As an organizational leadership and management consultant myself, I continue to struggle with growing my practice. My talents have afforded me a very lucrative career so far. But this has not come without sacrifice.

For over a decade, I averaged over 47,000 miles on the road a year. At one point, I was working with 8 different companies in 8 different locations at once! There was just no way to keep up that pace.

It was easy enough to outsource my infrastructure tasks such as administration, accounting, marketing and web work. But it was next to impossible to out-source my organizational leadership and management skills, because they are so unique.

The bottom line is for most consulting practices, we are only as good as our own talent. This means that our greatest value lies in experience and service and not usually in a product that can be mass-produced or a skill that can be easily taught.

The dilemma for me was, and continues to be, difficulty in growing my team. Unless I have other consultants who have the same or similar experience as myself, it's very hard to sub-contract other consultants out. As a result I am limited in the number of clients I can work with and the amount of total revenue my business can take in.

Said differently, it's very hard to scale my business and services. What makes my profession more challenging from the scaling up standpoint, is that what I provide as a service *is not technical or repeatable* like that of an IT or engineering expert. It has value precisely because it is not easy to learn. This makes what I provide as a service nearly impossible to scale, at least from the sub-contracting work side.

My situation is not unique. Other more well-known leadership consultants like Patrick Lencioni, Ken Blanchard, John Maxwell,

Marshall Goldsmith and Stephen Covey and Zig Ziglar before them have also faced the same dilemma. Unless they focused on something other than their unique talents, for example by creating a scalable training program or process, growing and scale their businesses was next to impossible.

For me, facing this challenge has meant asking how I can really grow my business. Looking 10 years into the future, there is no way I want to, or have the physical ability to stay on the road for years on end.

Yes, I would make a lot of money - but at what expense? I would certainly lose quality of life as the demands of physical travel built up on my body. I could even foresee eventually losing my family because I would never see them. And that is not going to happen.

Examining my leadership practice, I realized that the only way I could scale would be to expand my leadership training programs. This includes my coaching and consulting certification and my manager and executive coaching programs.

Beyond that, another way to scale my business is to make some of my expertise available through books, including this one that I'm writing.

Examining the "process variable" caused me to focus my growth strategy away from growing my consulting practice - a type of growth that was limited by time and my own personal capacity - and more on sharing and growing my "expertise footprint."

Other organizations with radically different business models may find themselves facing similar paradigm shifts when asking themselves "how can we grow most effectively in ways that accomplish our long-term goals?"

Here's an example of an organization that faced the same question:

One of the true limiters of a company's ability to grow lies in its' enterprise resource management (ERP) systems. Regardless of the revenue size of a company, ERP systems are complex, hairy beasts that are "pains in the ass" for everyone involved.

An ERP system combines both process and software to allow the entire infrastructure of a company to communicate and *manage data optimally*. When it works well, this is amazing: complex tasks, relationships, and optimizations can be performed automatically and in real-time.

But when it breaks down, it's a nightmare. Imagine trying to fix a complex, multi-system, interdependent automated logic system.

One of the things that makes ERP systems and their integration so complicated is the need to have all company processes, software, data and documentation all "singing to the same hymnal." Errors in code and technical specifications that most professionals might not even know are possible can make or break such systems.

It's an especially tall order when accounting, finance, IT, operations, marketing and sales have become accustomed to using their own processes and software, as often happens with companies that have gradually and organically adapted to the information age over the course of years or decades.

Getting a company onto a common ERP platform can take years and cost millions of dollars in labor, expertise, hardware, and software.

Yet without an ERP companies cannot continue to grow! Their ability to do business without ERP is limited by the ability of their workers to manually handle, communicate, and coordinate information. This ability always hits a ceiling eventually, no matter how numerous or skilled the personnel.

ERP's are a painful investment, but a necessary one for any company that wishes not to be limited in the amount of work it can handle.

I have personally been involved in a number of ERP resets. Serving as the company's expert facilitator, I've helped re-calibrate leadership, priorities, supplier relationships, and the processes involved for the completion of ERPs.

My involvement with one client was necessary because the situation had become very conflict-ridden, and the project was spiraling downhill at the rate of millions. Yet the company had to press forward because without a legitimate, functional and efficient

ERP system in place, there was no way the company could continue to grow.

Once you've examined and understood your strategic variables, you are well on your way to putting your strategies into action! You accomplish this by breaking down your strategic goals into concrete, actionable steps in a strategic roadmap.

Let's now examine a strategic roadmap formula that takes into account your objectives, goals, strategies, and metrics called the "OGSM."

Chapter 9

Developing Your OGSM Or 'Strategic Continuum'

Once your strategies are established, the real work of strategy begins; putting it into action, executing.

There are many ways to go about executing a strategy. The specific steps needed will be as varied as the strategies themselves, but a few time-tested systems have been established tracking your progress, measuring your outcomes, and help ensure your strategy's successful execution.

One of the best, simple execution templates is called an OGSM (Objectives, Goals, Strategies and Metrics). Though some sources state development of the OGSM came from Japan back in the 1950s, it is not clear where it really came from. Regardless, it is a framework that is widely used and adopted among Fortune 500 companies.[18]

This tried and true method is one of the best tools out there to take your strategy from an on-paper plan to the *execution* of a new reality for your organization.

Many great resources exist solely dedicated to OGSM, so I won't go too far into detail here. But here is a general overview of how OGSM works, and how it integrates with my own SAOL Strategic Continuum (pg. 56) for success:

Objective: Your objective is your overarching vision statement. It states what you'd like to achieve within the next 18-24 months. In this vision statement, ambition and timeline are critical. The vision

---

[18] Retrieved from https://archpointgroup.com/voice-of-the-leader-how-ogsm-has-helped-my-company/

must be realistically achievable within that time, but should not be so modest that complacency can set in.

Goals: What specific, measurable targets are you trying to hit? Market share growth? New industry penetration? Higher gross margins? Revenue? Be clear on what you'd like to achieve here. These goals must be measurable in some way so that you can verify whether or not you have achieved them, even if the method of verification is something seemingly subjective like customer satisfaction surveys.

Strategies: These are where you place your strategic initiatives, which we've discussed in detail in previous chapters.

Measures: What are your success criteria? What are your KPI's (Key Performance Indicators)? How will you know when you've reached your goals? When, and how frequently, will you collect data to assess your progress?

Objectives	Goals	Strategies	Metrics
What would you like to achieve within the next 18-24 months.	• What specific, measurable targets are you trying to hit? • Market share growth? • New industry penetration? • Higher gross margins? • Revenue? • Be clear on what you'd like to achieve here.	These are where you place your strategic initiatives, which we've discussed in detail in previous chapters.	• What are your success criteria? • What are your KPI's (Key Performance Indicators)? • How will you know when you've reached your goals? • When, and how frequently, will you collect data to assess your progress?

OGSM Chart Created by Rubi Ho

An OGSM provides the entire team with a strategic roadmap on one page. It allows the rest of the organization to easily:

1. Align their "sub-visions" (visions within individual departments and/or teams) with the big-picture goal of company-wide success.
2. Align "sub-strategies" to ensure synergy, not conflict, between teams and departments.
3. Create interdependencies within the company by establishing an organization-wide playbook.
4. Create a dashboard, physical or digital, that allows everyone to see and track progress.
5. Have a platform to drive productive work sessions by laying out exactly what needs to happen - and whether those goals are being met, or need intervention.

When done right, this results in the entire company being driven, integrated, and guided by the overarching Mission and Vision, Core Competencies, and Strategies.

I developed a 'one page' *integration* overview called the SAOL Integration Overview. It's simply another way to look at how to integrate a company's mission, vision and strategies throughout all vertical *and* horizontal 'layers' of a company.

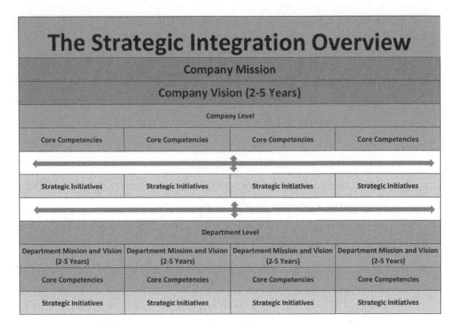

The Strategic Integration Overview

Company Mission			
Company Vision (2-5 Years)			
Company Level			
Core Competencies	Core Competencies	Core Competencies	Core Competencies
Strategic Initiatives	Strategic Initiatives	Strategic Initiatives	Strategic Initiatives
Department Level			
Department Mission and Vision (2-5 Years)	Department Mission and Vision (2-5 Years)	Department Mission and Vision (2-5 Years)	Department Mission and Vision (2-5 Years)
Core Competencies	Core Competencies	Core Competencies	Core Competencies
Strategic Initiatives	Strategic Initiatives	Strategic Initiatives	Strategic Initiatives

Created by Rubi Ho

Every Team Member Matters when it comes to Strategy

Let's say you're a warehouse worker. Why should you care about knowing your company's strategies?

You won't be making any department-level decisions. The only power you have is to ensure you are doing your job correctly and as efficiently as possible - right? So long as the company remains profitable and you do your job well enough to avoid attracting attention, why should you care about all of this "strategy" stuff?

In fact, it's very important for you to understand your company's mission, vision, and strategy. Not only for the company's sake, but also for your own.

I don't care if you are the paperclip pusher of the organization at the moment. The more you understand and know what it takes to win at work, the more empowered and more successful you will be in your career and in your life.

If you're working at an organization whose mission you believe in, understanding your company's mission, vision, and strategy will make your everyday labor meaningful to you. If you don't believe your company is doing anything good for the world, then your health might benefit from finding a job with an organization whose meaning you can believe in.

Even more than that, understanding your company's mission, vision, core competencies, and strategy will allow you to look for opportunities to improve on local processes. Being proactive in seeking or acting on opportunities to improve a company's strategy implementation is the fast track to promotional opportunities which can empower you in this job, and the next.

You never know - you could be a CEO in the making! You just have yet to be discovered. It's amazing what a small taste of initiative and strategic action can do for your whole career and life path.

Take this from a person who once was the "stamp licker" in the mailroom of an insurance company. I'm NOT kidding about that! Sure, I only lasted one day in that job because I quit. But that's beside the point. The point is, I never gave up on what I knew I could become. I knew I wanted power, freedom, and autonomy - and I got them!

If I had only known back then what I am writing about now, I could have saved myself many years of confusion and heartache that stemmed from being unsure how someone like me - an orphaned refugee, once a 'low-level worker' - could take command of my own life or work my way up the corporate ladder.

LIFE LESSON: NEVER GIVE UP ON YOUR PURSUIT TO THRIVE...EVER!

It is my hope that you will think and operate with a CEO mindset after reading this book, regardless of what your current job title or position is. I desire this not for the company's good, but for your own. *That* is what *thriving* is about!

You might not want to

> The skills that lead to winning are largely the same whether you're in business, community service, or personal fulfillment.

become the CEO of a large organization, and that's perfectly okay! But the same expertise in making decisions and accruing and wielding power that make a great CEO also empower you to reach any goal you may desire.

Once you see your company's mission, vision and strategies, once you *see* how all the departments are inter-connected and converge, then you begin to be able to take the sorts of actions that stand out.

Once you see what the company cares about, what its people care about, then you start to understand what the company needs to be successful.

You start to understand what the leaders need to be successful. You start to understand what teams need to be successful. And ultimately, what *you* need to be successful.

And then, you start to succeed. You start to generate "wins" for the company, wins for the leaders, wins for the teams, and of course, wins for *you*. The skills that lead to winning are largely the same whether you're in business, community service, or personal fulfillment.

Whether you are a self-employed freelancer, a retail cashier, or the CEO of a large organization, these principles and understandings can help you in your everyday life.

Chapter 10

Your Accountability around Strategy

Accountability is where many individuals and organizations stumble when implementing new strategies. The plan may look great on paper - but it's not getting implemented in the real world, and no one can agree on why or who is at fault.

Different individuals or departments may blame each other, or systemic factors outside of their control. There may not be a clear idea of how to solve the problem. What resources are needed, or is a change of team members the only solution?

The good news is, there is a way to promote accountability and ownership. When done properly, this ensures that all players have the *power* they need to get the job done - and the accountability to be unable to plausibly shift blame if the work subsequently doesn't happen.

Once you have your Mission, Vision, Strategies, Core Competencies and OGSM, you must have absolute clarity of who owns what.

While it's sometimes tempting to say "everyone is responsible for everything," this can lead to confusion over who is allowed or expected to perform certain duties, who has or hasn't been performing them, etc..

Some team members may even be afraid of "stepping on each other's toes" or "being too demanding" in asking for what they need to get the job done if they aren't explicitly authorized and charged with a specific outcome.

As is often said, "if everyone is accountable, no one is accountable." Actions and outcomes *must* eventually boil down to *one* individual.

Otherwise, without the "buck stopping" somewhere, there is a good chance that the ball may be dropped. It becomes easy to divert blame infinitely, or incorrectly, if things go wrong. In some cases, there might be genuine confusion or power struggles within a team who all believe *they* know best how to execute the strategy.

So if you're a CEO or strategy leader, don't be afraid to name specific people to take ownership of specific outcomes. There's no better way to ensure that the work gets done, and reduce friction from competing "leaders" at the same time.

If you're not in charge of delegating ownership, you may find yourself in a difficult situation when your decision-makers delegate a task to "everyone," or to multiple people, and failures and problems ensue.

The good news is, there's a way you can improve the situation and your reputation at the same time.

By stepping up and taking the blame when something goes wrong, you may feel you are exposing yourself to risk or blame. But you're actually doing two things:

1. Taking ownership of the initiative. When no one else is willing to do this, this makes you the default leader unless it's then assigned to another individual by your decision-makers.
2. Creating an immense feeling of relief in the CEO who usually just wants *someone* to take ownership. By demonstrating that you're willing to take blame, you're demonstrating that you're willing to take real responsibility for solving the problem.

100% of CEOs just want someone to take ownership of the situation, take the blame, and fix it. CEOs know that those who are successful are those who take responsibility for things going wrong instead of blaming circumstances beyond their control. The person who has that mindset will *always* be ahead of the pack.

Collaboration works up to a point. Eventually, we must be able to assign areas of ownership and accountability for the work that needs to be completed. Without clarity in ownership and accountability, we risk:

- Stepping on people's toes
- Repetitious and overlapping work
- Less than optimum focus on what needs to get done
- Work not getting done at all
- Lack of engagement
- Losing key people
- Losing the business
- Not being able to move to the next rung on our own career ladder

Spend the important time needed to determine who owns what and why. Let go of any idealistic ideas that "everyone" should be responsible for outcomes.

As you divide up the work, make sure you:

Assign the Right Strategies to the Right People

Who is best to lead the efforts? Who is best to complete specific tasks?

Make sure your people are not only capable, but also competent *and* have the bandwidth to complete the work. An employee who is already assigned more than forty hours of work per week likely won't be able to take on additional tasks without a skyrocketing error rate.

Get them personally involved and once assigned. Empower them by allowing them to map out their own work and strategies.

Take Time to Communicate Your Road Map and Strategy to Your Team

This is not an hour-long affair, but at least a half-day one!

Take the un-rushed, necessary time to give your team the entire context and 'why' of your strategies. Allow them to Q&A with you. Get them to a point where they both understand the strategies as much as you *and* own it.

Even better, consider coming up with the strategies together with your team so that they feel direct stake and ownership in the strategies' success.

This transparency is critical.

If team members do not truly understand the strategy or do not feel that their own knowledge, concerns, and questions were taken into account when creating it, they will have difficulty feeling enthusiasm and confidence for it. They may feel that the strategy is incomplete or flawed.

Even worse - if you do not consult relevant players when creating your strategy, you may really miss an important piece of information!

Tell Upper Management Who Owns What on Your Team and Why

This not only showcases your team members and gives them credit, but also shows management you are completely aligned with the overarching company initiatives as well.

Establish a Frequent and Firm Meeting Cadence with Your Team

Meetings for meetings' sake, especially informational meetings, are often useless. Simply getting everyone in the same room for no reason can lead to "attention fatigue," where team members are less engaged and alert in each meeting. This is sure to happen when meetings are held too frequently or are not useful enough.

Meetings to track and evaluate progress and troubleshoot problems, however, are *critical*.

Meetings that *actively engage* members by requiring them to present results and feedback have the opposite effect of passive listening meetings. The *best* way to promote a sense of team, ownership, and progress is to continually work towards and review your strategic initiatives, together.

Have the Guts to Hold People Accountable, Including Yourself

Almost 100% of strategies fail to meet a milestone, or need to be changed, at some point in the journey. This will happen because of some type of breakdown in process, people and/or performance.

> There will always be instances where facing people and/or performance issues will become sensitive. There will be times when you might have to 'fire' someone from your team because they aren't holding up their end of the stick. When this happens, you have to *own* this as a leader.

This makes the need for constant evaluation and problem-solving critical. Any obstacles must be overcome to reach your goal.

I can't tell you how many times I have been called in to "fix" a situation that occurred because candid, objective and transparent evaluations of a company's strategies weren't taking place. Because of lack of transparency, the strategy was stalled and no one in the organization could determine or agree upon what was needed to get it moving again.

With a strategic roadmap and objectives, goals, strategies and metrics in place however, there should be no excuse. Strategy leaders should be clearly named, and every strategy leader should be communicating about what's working, what's not, and what's needed to put things back on track.

There will always be instances where facing people and/or performance issues will become sensitive. There will be times when you might have to 'fire' someone from your team because they aren't holding up their end of the stick. When this happens, you have to *own* this as a leader.

What did *I* do or fail to do to make them successful? Did *I* make a mistake in estimating their skills, personality types, or resources? Are they going through something personal that is taking their mind off work?

Rarely are things genuinely "people problems" and not process problems. Bad policies will produce an abundance of "people problems," while good policies will make these rare.

But at times, every organization does encounter a genuine people problem. Someone isn't in the right seat on the bus, or isn't able to perform.

When this happens, take as much responsibility as you can to fix it. If the person can be helped, find the necessary resources or strategy for them and give them every opportunity to take advantage of these resources.

If the person needs to go, then help them exit the way you would want to be exited from the company. Do it like your father is in the room.

This sets you apart from the rest of the organization. Few companies do this properly and it shows in the culture of the organization. This is what shows the remaining employees that the core values are not just a pretty picture on the wall, but extend to the way the company handles everything, especially the bad experiences.

> People are the most important assets you can have. While you need cash in order to pay them and retain the best talent, it is indeed the talent, skill, dedication, enthusiasm, and innovation of your people which will determine what sort of experiences you deliver to your customers.

There might even be times when the strategy is just not working and needs to change. It's at these evaluation points that tough calls have to be made, lest you risk bringing the whole company under because you allowed things to carry on for too long without finding the source of the problem.

There are times when leadership fires people for the wrong or no reason. This is bad, not just for the employee who is fired - but because it means the company leadership is missing the true root of the problem they are trying to solve. And if they don't know what it is, they can't fix it.

When an organization faces repeated "people problems" with implementing its strategy, that's a good sign that the problems aren't actually with the people. Instead, there is likely some process, culture, or resource that needs to be improved to allow employees to meet their performance goals.

Yet there are also times when a team member who is not dedicated or capable is retained, simply because the leadership is afraid to take any negative action toward that employee.

I've known companies who held onto to their incompetent leaders to the demise of their strategies. Clearly the leader was the wrong fit to implement the strategy, yet because of the close relationships this leader had at the top, everyone chose to look the other way and *not* hold this person accountable for his failure to successfully implement the company's strategic objectives.

What happened to the strategy? In a word, after millions of resources were invested in it, nothing.

Don't let this happen to your strategy!

We've ended this chapter on a note about people. People are the most important assets you can have. While you need cash in order to pay them and retain the best talent, it is indeed the talent, skill, dedication, enthusiasm, and innovation of your people which will determine what sort of experiences you deliver to your customers.

Now that I've got you focusing on how to thrive on the business side of things at work, **let's take a deep dive into how you thrive and win on the relationship and leadership side of your career or business**.

Chapter 11

How to Win in Relationships & Leadership (Start with Warmth and Competence)

It's no secret that departments and leaders within organizations don't always get along. Because they have different expertise and are charged with different responsibilities, it's easy for them to develop opposing ideas about what's best for the company as a whole. All parties think they are doing the right thing - but they may not have access to the whole story.

We can end up with a scene that looks like The Jets vs The Sharks, straight out of West Side Story. The result of poor communication and relationships can be that entire departments are at odds with one another and competing for limited resources.

Conversely, there are scenarios where an entire division is completely converged and aligned. These groups communicate their priorities, resulting in top notch delivery, a high sense accomplishment, and a positive culture.

Both scenarios have company-wide impact.

The latter scenario of alignment is what *every organization* should strive for. Even beyond a sense of harmony and warmth between employees, departments that are aligned to the most complete version of the big picture available simply deliver better results.

Winning with your stakeholders is most likely when you ensure that there are *positive and productive* relationships with *everyone* you are associated with, in the workplace.

Everyone you may ask? Yes, *everyone!*

If there are leaders in the organization who don't support

all employees in the organization, their fitness to lead needs to be evaluated. Just as a body needs all its organs to remain healthy, an organization needs all of its departments and team members to deliver great performance.

If a leader is hostile or indifferent to certain parts of the body they belong to, they probably should not be making decisions about how the body functions.

When was the last time you met someone new, and within nanoseconds, had a sense about whether you could trust her or him? What was the perception that caused you to make that assessment? How did they create a feeling of trust or distrust so quickly?

You may not even know, because social perceptions are often very subtle. We can rarely express matters of body language or micro-expressions (expressions that flit across a person's face so quickly we may not even consciously remember seeing them) in words.

When it comes to your work life, you intuitively know that you are *most* productive when you have *trusting* and credible relationships with your teammates. Trusting and credible relationships encourage partnerships and support, and reduce any skepticism or doubt that might interfere with progress.

Several years ago there was a study done at Harvard Business School called **"The Dynamics of Warmth and Competence Judgments and their Outcomes in Organizations."** The researchers were, Amy J. C. Cuddy, Peter Glick, and Anna Beninger.

The researchers found that, when new people encounter each other, they almost immediately make a determination on whether the other should be trusted. That determination is made primarily on two categories:

- A perception of **'warmth,'** which could be expressed as care and support for other people, and
- A perception of **'competence,'** which could be expressed as skill and ability to do one's job with a high degree of excellence.

Both need to be perceived in order for a person to be trusted.[19] Those perceptions become especially crucial when taking care of stakeholders, where one decision-maker is charged with making decisions, not just for themselves, but for others.

Our most important judgements related to people in business, then, are based on whether we perceive people as **warm** *and* **competent.**

A **warm** person is friendly towards other people, respecting them and caring for them. With such warmth they create a reciprocal liking, trust and bonding. People believe that a warm person will help or support them if they need it, so they are more likely to support the warm and caring person in turn.

In contrast, a **cold** person has a lot more difficulty gaining sympathy from others. Those who are perceived as cold are those who don't seem to care about other people's feelings or well-being. Their apparent indifference or hostility toward other people's welfare leads new acquaintances to conclude that they would not help or support them in a time of need. As a result, they are less likely to trust this person as a partner, and less likely to help or support them.

Several factors play into whether a person is viewed as warm or cold. People who seem impatient with others may be perceived as cold, for example, while those who take time to get to know people are more likely to be perceived as warm. For this reason, business leaders, who demand efficiency and results, are often stereotyped as "cold."

> **When you accomplish both warmth and competence in the eyes of your business peers, you accomplish something very important. You are now someone who they not only enjoy working with - but someone they believe is a high performer.**

People who have difficulty showing interest in others due to shyness or cultural differences may also be seen as "colder" than those who are comfortable talking and asking questions, making "out

[19] Cuddy AJC, Glick P, Beninger A. The dynamics of warmth and competence judgments, and their outcomes in organizations. *Research in Organizational Behavior.* 2011;31:73-98. doi:10.1016/j.riob.2011.10.004.

group" people - people who are not familiar members of the same groups as those making the judgements - more vulnerable to being considered "cold."

When we understand this, it becomes easy to learn some skills and techniques for ensuring that others know we really care about them - even if there might be obstacles such as shyness, unfamiliarity, or a need for us to make tough calls and get efficient results.

But we don't *just* need to be seen as warm to be trusted as a business partner. A sweet little old lady who has no business skills may fill your heart with joy, but you're unlikely to put her on your board of directors. We must also be seen as competent - as highly skilled operators who can deliver great results.

If a person is seen as competent, they may be admired or sought out as a business partner, even if they are also perceived as cold or hostile. Likewise, if a person is perceived as warm but incompetent, they're unlikely to be offered a leadership position or a big salary.

Here again, some stereotypes can come into play - fair or otherwise.

People may be viewed as incompetent if they act indecisive or uncertain. They may also be viewed as incompetent if they don't fit in with their society's standards of "businesslike" behavior as far as the clothes they wear, their body language, and their social etiquette.

When you accomplish both warmth and competence in the eyes of your business peers, you accomplish something very important. You are now someone they not only enjoy working with - but who they also believe is a high performer.

Warmth + Competence = Admiration + Trust

Both warmth and competence are both factors that we like and so it is easy to admire people who have both.

Warmth *without* competence however, can lead to a person being liked - but not respected or trusted with power. It is easy to feel superior to people who appear incompetent and sometimes we may even have a subconscious drive to see others as incompetent in order to feel better about our own skills. For those who feel insecure about their own abilities, pity may allow them to feel that they themselves are "warm" but also more competent than others.

Competence is important - but it doesn't guarantee that a person will be liked, admired, or sought after as a business partner. There are two important points that I hope you will take away from this section:

1. If you want people to admire you, you must give a perception of both **warmth** and **competence.**

   If this means learning specific social skills such as conversational skills, etiquette, body language training, or the "rules" of business attire, so be it. Being perceived as warm and competent is worth overcoming any innate shyness or cultural differences you may have when entering the business world.

   Of course, you must also be good at the services you offer as a business partner! You won't be able to "fake" competence for very long, so make sure you can really deliver on any promises you make.

2. You must also be cautious with your judgement. When evaluating others, be careful out of your automatic conclusions around **warmth** and **competence**.

   Take time to truly understand these judgements in yourself, rather than quickly classifying and dismissing them. You may find that your opinions are incorrectly swayed by matters which are not accurate representations of character or skill, such as the other person's shyness, cultural background, or wardrobe.

   It's always better to have the partner who *really cares* and can *really deliver* rather than the one who says all the right things and looks the part but actually lacks skills or care for the organization.

No one is perfect. None of us have the bandwidth to have great relationships with *everyone* on the planet. But when it comes to our working relationships, we *must,* and I do mean *must,* strive for creating and maintaining healthy working relationships with everyone we interact with frequently.

After all, we all work better when we feel good about the people we work *with*. We enjoy our work a lot more when we genuinely care about these people, too!

All **employees need to cultivate these skills of warmth, competence, and positive relationships in order to achieve optimal outcomes.**

This includes Presidents, CEOs, and Owners. In fact, it is *especially* people in these positions who will experience the greatest success if they are perceived as warm and competent by both their employees and the public.

Spend the time to get to know your organization and its people. If your people feel that you really care about them, they will reciprocate by doing everything they can to make sure that your organization runs smoothly.

They will have your back, and they will make sure you are aware of any issues that are starting to bubble up. They will also be more likely to trust that you will make the best decisions for the organization if they give you accurate information about what's happening on the ground. This, in turn, will increase your ability to be informed and effective.

Let's take a more detailed look at how to create healthy, win-win working relationships, and with whom!

Chapter 12

Winning with Relationships at Work

It can be easy to feel as though work relationships are just as important as family relationships. In rare cases this might be true – especially if you and your workmates have been through a lot together.

For the most part however, your working relationships will *never* be as close as your familial ones.

Why am I opening with this point? Because many of us sacrifice our familial relationships for our work relationships. The nature of work, with its demands and hours, require that we do whatever we need to do to stay successful in our jobs. This means we are at work much more than we are at home.

> **Later in this book, we'll discuss my Life Map method for maximizing well-being at home and in one's personal life**

This leads to several problems.

For one, we feel guilty about this. We end up feeling resentful of the lack of time we have for our personal lives, while at the same time feeling powerless to change this. We also end up taking negative feedback at work or career changes much more personally – sometimes devastatingly so.

Here's a profound thought: I firmly believe that we *subconsciously* know that *we are spending time away from our family* while at work. And whenever things go "wrong" at work, we take it out on *everyone* around us because of this hidden resentment. This can be made even worse if we take problems at work personally because we are approaching work relationships like personal relationships.

When we treat work like a place for relationships instead of results, we end up misaligned both at work and at home. If we don't take control of this through conscious choices, it can ruin our experiences of both family life and work.

Later in this book, we'll discuss my Life Map method for maximizing well-being at home and in one's personal life. But for now – what is the *right* way to "win at" work relationships, if the goals and rules that govern these are totally different from our home relationships?

We *need* positive relationships at work. That is an absolute fact – not just for personal satisfaction reasons, but for team performance reasons.

For all the countless times I've helped teams realign their strategies and focus, I've probably dealt with at least three times more cases where teams and leaders needed my help to rekindle their broken relationships.

Hostility, jealousy, personal dislike, and any number of other personal feelings can happen when work relationships go wrong. These can destroy a team's ability to meet financial goals just as quickly as an actual lack of physical resources or cashflow can.

After all, *everyone's* performance at work depends on the members of the team working like a well-oiled machine. Personal resentments and attachments alike can "gum up" the works by taking our eyes off our shared goal and onto differences in how we feel about different workmates.

The goal for work relationships is this: mutual professional respect. Remember, you aren't members of a family: you're players of a game. You may like or dislike each other for personal reasons, but at the end of the day you're all on the field for one reason: to win. That should be the frame through which you see your work relationships, since it's certainly the way management views you.

Take a look at the short list below of a few ways that work relationships can become 'broken,' and how business is impacted if one or more of these conditions exist.

What	How it slows down or impedes progress
Strongly held biases	Unwillingness to change or try something different, even if current situation is not working. Can be fatal in a changing market requiring new approaches.
Inflexibility or stubborn actions	Lack of collaboration and teamwork leading to disarray and non-efficient progress. Like a cog that's jammed in a machine, one person or relationship can derail an entire strategy's execution.
Loyalty to people over objectivity	Subjective judgment versus objective judgment when making decisions. Can lead to players being kept or dismissed for reasons unrelated to their performance or results.
Being overly fearful	Creates state of hesitancy around actions and eliminates propensity to take necessary risk. Fear of change in a changing market can be just as bad as recklessness.
Acting as if you "know it all"	Shuts down the rest of the room because they have to be the "smartest." Prevents potentially useful ideas from being brought to the table or acted upon.

Intimidating behavior, known or unknown	Shuts down and disengages team members. Guarantees lack of active engagement later in the project.
Complacency	Engagement, ownership and production are next to zero. Feeling that change "isn't really necessary" can be fatal in a changing market.
Over displaying people pleasing	Says "yes" to everything which is NOT necessarily a good thing! Every player's discerning judgment is needed for optimal results.
Appearing too title and power hungry	Destroys potential for relationships because "it's all about me." May even create the impression that business results are secondary to personal results, resulting in resistance from other team members.
Prideful	Creates un-productive collaboration. Ego-first players can easily shut out useful ideas.
Over analytical Too technical	Shuts down and disengages the room because everyone is lost. All players must understand the "how" and "why" to be engaged in optimizing it regardless of department or specialty.

Too emotional	Objectivity is questioned, breeding lack of trust. Are this person's ideas based on facts, or non-factual opinions?

Created by Rubi Ho

Any single factor above can stop a team's progress, and therefore a company's strategy and/or performance, in its tracks. Have you ever dealt with, or *been* one or more of the above?

Most of us have been both the recipient and the giver of issues like these at some point in our professional careers. Because of a lack of education around what constitutes healthy work relationships, it's easy for us to get wrapped up in our own egos, or our personal like or dislike of other players, rather than staying wrapped up in our shared professional goals.

Relationship management, like business management, can be very complex. Let's look at some critical people you need to ensure you have healthy relationships with in order to ensure your professional and business success.

STAKEHOLDER RELATIONSHIPS

Do you know who all of your stakeholders are?

Imagine we are on top of Mount Everest together. The winds are gusting over 200 mph. You try to pitch a tent and realize you don't have *any* stakes to hold it down! Instead, your team agrees to take turns and be *human stakes* for your tent, holding down the corners of your tent, so you can be sheltered throughout the night!

Now think about this: what would give them the motivation to do this, even risking their lives for you?

I define a "stakeholder" as someone who is dependent on you to provide her with excellent service and/or products in a "servant leadership-oriented" way.

This means that you lead by serving: you set yourself up as an authority and a provider who is trusted with power *precisely because* your driving motivation is the well-being and best interest of the people you lead and serve. When leadership and service become one in the same, you have an uncrackable leadership model.

When you do this, your stakeholder will go the extra mile for *you* as well when it is their turn!

In my case, I can't tell you the number of new engagements I've received simply from word of mouth. This is because my clients recognize that I have their best interests at hear and I use my authority and expertise to advance their best interests.

My motto is very simple: "Treat the person in front of me as if she is the most important person in the world to me."

That motto has led to me having many loyal clients, and has afforded me the blessing of not having to do a lot of marketing for myself.

Treating your stakeholders as the most important people on earth will go a long way toward helping you not only build your working relationships, but also helping you create win-win situations for all parties involved.

Remember: it is by the quality of your *results* for your stakeholders that you will be known. This means that the better your results, the better the deals you will be offered by future clients or employers.

Let's take a look at a few critical stakeholders you *most* need to have healthy working relationships with.

Your Boss

"Bad relationship with a manager" continues to be one of the primary reasons people leave their jobs.[20] Often egos become involved, and one or both parties in a boss-employee relationship make decisions based on ego rather than on the best results for the company. That's NOT going to change any time soon.

However, this means that if we can be effective at cultivating good relationships with our bosses, we can eliminate *most of the reasons we will ever have to leave a job.* Needless to say, this makes our work life much less stressful.

At the very least, put some effort and people skills research into making your relationship with your boss work.

Remember: it's not about whether you like them personally, or vice versa. It's about *results*. If both of you can keep this in mind, you can likely develop a healthy working relationship even if you might personally rub each other the wrong way.

If and only if that approach doesn't work, leave. But not before then!

Contrary to what we may tell ourselves, *the grass is NOT always greener on the other side!* If we have irreconcilable issues with one boss and we cannot learn to manage these, chances are very good we will run into the same situation in a future job.

All workers, including our bosses, carry lots and lots of personal baggage into the professional arena. We all have biases, insecurities,

---

[20] Schwantes, M. (2017, September 21). Why Do Employees Really Quit Their Jobs? Research Says It Comes Down to These Top 8 Reasons. Retrieved from https://www.inc.com/why-do-employees-really-quit-their-jobs-research-says-it-comes-down-to-these-top-8-reasons.html

fears, and emotional needs that we may misplace onto our work relationships. For that reason, "the perfect boss" is very rare.

Short of us going to work in a cave or joining a monastery, (I'll bet there are people issues there as well) we aren't going to be able to escape dealing with imperfect people, including bosses!

Suck it up! Deal with it! Give it your best shot!

One thing we *can* do is make sure that *we* stay results-oriented. We can have professional respect for our boss even if we might not choose to invite them to a dinner party.

After all, it takes two to tango – and we can't personally change our bosses' behavior, but we can change our own. The only way we can influence them is to lead by example: if we remain staunchly results-focused, there's a possibility they may as well.

Trust me: it is always tough to start over in a new job. Moving to a new position may mean supplanting your family, your standard of income, acclimating to a new environment, a new culture, and proving our credibility all over again for a new group of people. It can be very complicated and risky!

Of course, you can't control anyone else's behavior. If you have a boss that insists on letting personal issues take precedence over team results, that's not your fault. But it's always worth doing all you can to make it work – unless you really want to start over in a new job for other reasons, such as career fit or better leveraging your own core competencies.

How Can You Develop a Great Relationship with Your Boss?

Here are some solid ways to avoid personal conflicts and keep your boss focused on the quality of your results:

Be clear on the expectations of your role and meet these expectations. To accomplish this, ask questions like:

1. What are the measures of success?
2. Who does your boss consider to be key stakeholders connected to your role?

3. What does the boss expect to see from you on a daily, weekly, and monthly basis?
4. How often does she/he want you to communicate with her/him?
5. What does he/she *really* want to know/not know from you?
6. Establishing the answers to these questions immediately – and then meeting them – can save you immense trouble.

Understand what the boss values and is motivated by. Ask questions like:

1. What professionally motivates the boss?
2. What personally motivates the boss?
3. What does the boss *really* value? How do you know?
4. What's her/his leadership style?

Understanding this can help you to cultivate a harmonious relationship with your boss, and receive harmony and support in return.

Proactively "Own" Your Role to Make Your Boss Look Good

When your boss makes you look good, she looks good as your skilled and competent supervisor. Likewise, when you make your boss look good, you'll also look good as a stellar member of her high-performing team!

Some of us might be thinking, 'what if my boss takes all of the credit and still manages to make me look bad?'

Remember what I started saying in this section? Do all of the 'right things' first. If you still don't see things moving in the right direction, leave! But not until you've done all you can to cultivate skills that will lead to success in your next job.

Most times, when we do what we need to do to take care of our boss, things work out in our favor. If things don't go well even though we've done all the right things, the worst that can happen is that we've now cultivated strong performance and relationship skills under challenging circumstances. This will make us that much stronger in our next role.

Worse case, if you feel like you *have* to leave your company because things aren't working out, make sure you use *it* to its full potential to get the results you personally need. Maximize any relationships, recommendations, and other perks before making your best next move. At the very least, you deserve it.

Understand The Relationship of Your Boss to Her Boss

Your boss's boss is one of your critical stakeholders. You may not report directly into him or her, but your boss *does* report to their boss about the results achieved by your team. And that is all you need to know!

The reality is there is a "pecking order" in business. Having to report to someone *does not stop* at *any* level. No matter who your boss is, there is always someone she has to please. Understanding who that is, and why, can help you optimize your relationship with her, and your next step if you have to move on.

A manager reports to a Senior Manager, who reports to a Director, who reports to a Senior Director. Even the CEO reports to the Board, who report to the Stockholder or Executive Chair.

In most companies, even a CEO needs to worry about getting 'fired' if they don't get results that please the stockholders. So understanding what the stockholders want – and how the CEO can accomplish that – can help you do your job, *and* please the CEO.

Get the point? The more we are aware of what's expected by *everyone*, inclusive of our boss's boss, the better we will be at taking care of our boss, and ultimately our own position and reputation.

A word of wisdom: Make it a point to have an understanding of what your boss's boss is expecting from your boss and ensure your communication, work and priorities properly align to those expectations!

This doesn't just make your boss look good: it makes your team and everyone on it look good too!

Appreciate the Underappreciated Roles

How often do we take time daily to appreciate those who support our organization?

What did you do today for the people who *didn't* report directly to you? It's the bare minimum of your job description to support your own team as a leader, but did you also support people NOT on your team?

If you did, that's called 'character.' If you didn't that's called "smoke and mirrors," and it *will* cause problems down the line.

Your administrative assistants, cleaning crew, help desk and front desk staff, and other "back office" people may not be viewed as the most glamorous workers in your organization. But they are absolutely essential.

Where would you be without them? Not in a very good place. Who determines the average consumer's impression of your company's quality, personality and character? They do!

These are your stakeholders too. They have a stake in having a healthy organization. They also know who ignores them and who treats them like the *important* people that they are. They know whether they *like* the organization they work for or whether they are just doing the bare minimum to pay the bills.

All relationships are mutual, and a company's treatment of its "lowest level" workers – who make up the majority of its workforce – often determines their level of performance for the company in turn.

I work with many people who are "important" by title and responsibility. I work with CEOs, experts, and multi-million dollar salespeople.

But for that very reason, I recognize that the "back office" people are *just* as important! And this has big results – both for my own career, and for the results I'm able to obtain for my client companies.

There have been countless times where administrative assistants have gone the extra mile for me, with amazing results. It's amazing what "non-managerial" employees can do when they are motivated to be creative and extra-diligent.

I like to believe that I obtain these results because I treat all workers the same: as *very important people!*

Remember, before we had any sort of career or title, we were a human being. We should treat everyone in the organization with respect.

And that isn't just an ideal. It's a strategy for whole-company success.

Succeeding in Peer Relationships

I've dealt with toxic relationships between business peers which have delayed or threatened multi-million dollar projects.

How is it possible that interpersonal relationships could threaten such huge amounts of money? It's easy when peers don't align on:

- Priorities
- Timelines
- Budgets
- Ownership
- Processes
- Roles and responsibilities
- Personality differences
- Mentoring
- Communication styles
- Work styles

Indeed, the roots of differences of opinion about strategy – which can often lead to non-execution of strategy – are often interpersonal. When peers don't trust each other's judgment or have personal resentment toward each other, this can manifest as drastic challenges to strategy implementation.

This is only a subset of a much longer list of ways that peers can be misaligned on (see my previous book, "Many Parts, One Body").

To avoid impacting organizational performance, we must be proactive in fostering healthy relationships with our peers. We don't have to love them – but we must recognize their professional skills, and be willing to work together toward shared goals.

Have you ever had any sort of peer conflict? Yes, I am being facetious. Of course you have – we all have. And that's exactly my point.

Any type of relationship is prone to conflict. Personal conflicts can never be entirely eliminated from any task which involves people. The best that we can hope for is to drastically reduce peer conflicts by focusing on business goals together – allowing us to temporarily set aside any personal issues for mutual shared gain.

So what sorts of things can we focus on that will allow us to transcend our personal differences?

- Our business. The mission, values, strategies, and core competencies of our business. Our own personal roles and contributions, upon which our salaries and reputations depend.
- And our *business relationships*. Remember – you don't have to be best friends to form an efficient and praiseworthy business team. When you focus on your professional strengths and skills – you may just start to like each other more.

Peers are people who are your "equivalents," whether by title, responsibility and/or key partnerships in the business. They're neither your bosses nor your subordinates, but rather your teammates who must work together to accomplish your team goal.

Unhealthy relationships with these stakeholders can stop business from progressing, reinforce silos, and build toxicity. Stakeholder relationships at the peer level are absolutely critical for Organizational Health. If your teams don't function, then nothing functions.

Peers also play a big part in our own ongoing career success.

There's a saying: "Be careful how you treat people on the way up because they are the same people you will pass on the way down." One day, these peers of yours might be people who report to you, *or you to them!*

In either case, your professional reputation will depend on their willingness to work with you toward shared goals.

So what can you do? Simple: Treat your peers as you would like to be treated. Or better yet, find out how they want to be treated, and treat them that way.

One of the best ways to win with your peers is to avoid what I call "Smeagol Syndrome."

- Just like the character in Lord of the Rings who transforms from a friendly hobbit into a murderous monster through obsession with the Ring, we all have possessions, thoughts and opinions that we consider to be "my precious."

It's normal and healthy to have things that bring us joy, or projects whose outcomes we are very invested in. At times, though, we can obsess and hoard them at the expense of our relationships. We may unwittingly make team members feel unwanted, excluded, or untrusted in our passionate pursuit of perfection.

Like Smeagol, we "hoard it" and even "kill for it," sometimes at the expense of our business relationships. When we treat peers as though we don't want their help or don't want them around, there's a good chance they'll treat us the same way in the future. And that could become a serious problem.

So what can we focus on to create win-win scenarios with our peers? Here's a short list of options:

The Organization's Overarching Vision and Priorities

Another way of saying this is: "win together!"

Elevate your focus to the big-picture level that makes *both* yours and your peers' personal priorities secondary. This will make you *both* look beyond the functions you lead, and toward the outcomes of the whole operation. It will also take away the propensity to protect "your piece of the pie."

Admittedly, this can be hard to do if there is not unity in the senior leadership arena. If this example is not being set by department leaders, department team members may have to work extra hard to learn about and learn how to contribute to the company-wide visions on their own.

Develop a Genuine Relationship with Your Peers

The *best* working relationships we will ever have in the workplace are where we have *both* professional *and personal* relationships with our peers. We don't have to have them over for dinner every weekend, but we can still enjoy their company and get to know about their personal lives.

When we understand who the people are that we work with, we are able to connect and relate on a human level. This builds trust, confidence, and camaraderie.

Help Your Peers Win, First!

Zig Ziglar said it best: "You can get anything you want in life so long as you help enough people get what they want!"

Sometimes a team isn't ready to win together and most members may be preoccupied with their individual goals. Someone on the team must be the first person to put the team's goals first and demonstrate that your team's shared goals are the most important.

You be that person!

We mentioned earlier the model of servant-leadership: the leader who is trusted precisely *because* they look out for everyone's goals.

Push your team up first, and be the last one down with the ship while making sure everyone else is safe. When people know they are safe with you, they will go above and beyond for your shared goals.

If we could all be more like Ernest Shackleton, who gave his only food rations to sick crew members when the expedition he led went wrong, our business would always be successful and no one would ever want to leave.

What To Do in Times of Peer Conflict

Peer conflicts *will* occur wherever there are peers. Peer conflicts can feel extremely sensitive and completely out of your control. All the good intentions in the world might not be able to stop interpersonal differences from blowing up, or solidifying into a stumbling block.

When this is the case, get help and seek solutions outside of yourself. You might reach a point where you are too close to the situation to see or think objectively anymore. The personal and/or professional biases might be too strong. Thoughts of incompetence, or dislike are difficult to overcome – and can be deadly to strategy implementation if you must continue working with a person who you distrust or simply don't want to work with.

Peer biases *must* be resolved because of what they mean for organizational progress. Organizational Health requires teams who *can* and *will* work efficiently and harmoniously together, regardless of personal history.

These peer issues, if allowed to persist without address or resolution, will implode and take a negative toll on business, team, and individual performance.

Who Resolves Toxic Situations Among Peers?

Some organizations may have designated people within their human resources departments who are charged with mediating personal conflicts. Others may put this duty by default onto the team members' bosses, or hire external experts when they realize that a situation is impeding company performance.

Here are a few types of mediators you may wish to reach out to, and some pros and cons of each:

Strong External Leadership and Management Consultants

Consultants are strong choices *if and only if* they have the expertise *and* have embraced *and* been embraced by the organization and its culture.

On one hand, as specialists they provide finely honed skills and outside, objective viewpoints on what is best for the company. On the other hand, as outsiders, they may not fully understand the company's goals or culture the same way an internal HR department might.

It is worth calling in external consultants when internal parties have not been able to resolve a conflict. But have a plan in place to ensure that the consultant truly understands the company's mission, values, goals, and culture; and to ensure that their recommendations are followed-up with by internal accountability holders after the consultant has left.

Strong HR Business Partners

Internal HR partners who are strategists are great resources if they are given leadership authority, respected by the impacted parties, and possess the appropriate skills.

HR departments may have difficulty resolving conflicts, however, if they are not given much authority or training by company leadership. Both expertise and the ability to make important decisions are necessary for conflict resolution mediators to be effective.

The Peers' Bosses

Because a boss is ultimately responsible for the performance of the team they oversee, conflict resolution often falls on bosses by default.

This can work well if the bosses are given sufficient expertise, training, authority, and bandwidth to successfully resolve the conflict. But if they are not given the skills of conflict resolution, the power to make important decisions, and the time to devote to personnel conflicts, an outside party may be necessary.

Company-Level Decision Makers

Leaders who can literally 'move people off of the bus' are needed in some cases. There are scenarios where the *only* way the peer conflict is resolved is by removing or relocating the peer causing the problem.

Some peer conflicts arise because of genuine performance problems or skill mismatches for the job. Not everyone can be turned into a top performer in the job title they were hired into. In extreme cases, the decision makers need to *both* set the expectations of proper peer-to-peer relations and draw the line of tolerance for subpar performance or disruptive behavior.

Once that line is crossed, that person or *those* individuals causing the problem need to go!

The External Customer Relationship

External stakeholders are the people who benefit from what your organization does. These can include board members, product or service customers you provide work to, and even people in the community who influence or do business with your company.

Organizations tend to do a pretty good job of taking care of their external customers because external customers are where their revenue ultimately comes from. When corporate decision-makers have their eyes focused on the dollar amount, the external customer tends to be the first person they think of.

When revenues are down, business leaders instinctively know to ask: "How do we improve the customer experience? How do we offer them more value, or help them to understand our value better?"

The same questions are not always asked regarding internal relationships like those listed above, but they should be!

While your external customers are *very* important, your internal relationships are just as important, if not more so. The most customer-oriented CEO will not be able to deliver great customer service if all of their workers are unhappy and un-invested in the success of the company.

Internal relationships are the relationships you depend upon to get the work done. This includes production, customer service, etc.. Problems with internal relationships will manifest directly as problems for the customers – whether you realize it or not.

When times get hard, or external customers aren't happy, it is your internal stakeholders who you must work with to turn things around.

One great way to turn things around when customers are unhappy is to use a VOC (voice of customer) communication or survey to determine what went wrong and make it right.

This sounds easy, and it really is. But you may find that your customers direct you right back to your internal relationships: why are your customer support staff unhappy or untrained? Why is your marketing ineffective or your sales staff lackluster?

The answer: *internal* relationships. Someone on your team internally is feeling unappreciated, undervalued, uninvested, or distrustful of other people within your organization.

As a leader, it falls on you to do all you can to fix this. If you don't, your organization will not succeed.

Your Relationship With Your Family

Yes, your family definitely belongs in this section!

Your family is a critical component of your professional success. Leave your family out of this picture and you might as well become single now, because it's NOT going to work out in the long run!

My 10-year-old son (age during the writing of this book) does not care how my work day went, nor will he ever ask me about what I accomplished during the day! My wife is the same way. They **simply** want *my attention on the family!* They want the same kind of love and support from me that I receive from them.

After all this talk of business, finance, and bottom lines, it may be difficult to shift gears and see where our families fit in. The story below is an excellent illustration of that invaluable, ineffable value that our families give to us – and which we want to strive to give to our families.

THE RABBI'S GIFT

This story concerns a monastery that had fallen upon hard times. Once a great order, as a result of waves of anti-monastic persecution in the seventeenth and eighteenth centuries and the rise of secularism in the nineteenth, all its branch houses were lost and it had become decimated.

There were only five monks left in the decaying mother house: an abbot and four others, all over seventy in age. Clearly it was a dying order.

In the deep woods surrounding the monastery there was a little hut that a rabbi from a nearby town occasionally used for a hermitage. Through their many years of prayer and contemplation the old monks had become a bit psychic, so they could always sense when the rabbi was in his hermitage. "The rabbi is in the woods, the rabbi is in the woods again," they would whisper to each other.

As he agonized over the imminent death of his order, it occurred to the abbot to visit the hermitage and ask the rabbi if by some slim chance he could offer advice that might save the monastery.

The rabbi welcomed the abbot into his hut. But when the abbot explained the purpose of his visit, the rabbi could only commiserate with him.

"I know how it is," he exclaimed. "The spirit has gone out of the people. It is the same in my town. Almost no one comes to the synagogue anymore."

So the old abbot and the old rabbi wept together. Then they read parts of the Torah and quietly spoke of deep things. The time came when the abbot had to leave. They embraced each other.

"It has been a wonderful thing that we should meet after all

these years, "the abbot said, "but I have still failed in my purpose for coming here. Is there nothing you can tell me, no piece of advice you can give me that would help me save my dying order?"

"No, I am sorry," the rabbi responded. "I have no advice to give. The only thing I can tell you is that the Messiah is one of you."

When the abbot returned to the monastery his fellow monks gathered around him to ask, "Well what did the rabbi say?"

"He couldn't help," the abbot answered. "We just wept and read the Torah together. The only thing he did say, just as I was leaving --it was something cryptic-- was that the Messiah is one of us. I don't know what he meant."

In the days and weeks and months that followed, the old monks pondered this and wondered whether there was any possible significance to the rabbi's words. The Messiah is one of us?

"Could he possibly have meant one of us monks here at the monastery?" The monks asked themselves. "If that's the case, which one?

"Do you suppose he meant the abbot? Yes, if he meant anyone, he probably meant Father Abbot. He has been our leader for more than a generation.

"On the other hand, he might have meant Brother Thomas. Certainly Brother Thomas is a holy man. Everyone knows that Thomas is a man of light.

"Certainly he could not have meant Brother Elred! Elred gets crotchety at times. But come to think of it, even though he is a thorn in people's sides, when you look back on it, Elred is virtually always right. Often very right. Maybe the rabbi did mean Brother Elred.

"But surely not Brother Phillip. Phillip is so passive, a real nobody. But then, almost mysteriously, he has a gift for somehow always being there when you need him. He just magically appears by your side. Maybe Phillip is the Messiah.

"Of course the rabbi didn't mean me. He couldn't possibly have meant me. I'm just an ordinary person. Yet supposing he did? Suppose I am the Messiah? O God, not me. I couldn't do that much for You, could I?"

As they contemplated in this manner, the old monks began to treat each other with extraordinary respect on the off chance that one among them might be the Messiah. And on the off chance that each monk himself might be the Messiah, they began to treat themselves with extraordinary respect.

Because the forest in which it was situated was beautiful, it so happened that people still occasionally came to visit the monastery to picnic on its tiny lawn, to wander along some of its paths, even now and then to go into the dilapidated chapel to meditate. As they did so, without even being conscious of it, they sensed the aura of extraordinary respect that now began to surround the five old monks and seemed to radiate out from them and permeate the atmosphere of the place.

There was something strangely attractive, even compelling, about it. Hardly knowing why, the people began to come back to the monastery more frequently to picnic, to play, to pray. They began to bring their friends to show them this special place. And their friends brought their friends.

Then it happened that some of the younger men who came to visit the monastery started to talk more and more with the old monks. After a while one asked if he could join them. Then another. And another. So within a few years the monastery had once again become a thriving order and, thanks to the rabbi's gift, a vibrant center of light and spirituality in the realm.

LIFE LESSON: Simply focus on treating *every* single one of your people 'as if they are the Messiah.' The rest, so they say, will take care of itself.

Maximizing the Team Relationship

I've saved the Team Relationship section for last because the team relationship is the most complicated. Apart from your boss, it's your team members with whom you will spend the *most* time with at work. They truly feel like and become your "work family."

As with *any* family, there are pluses and minuses. There are quirky personalities and those you prefer not to have at the dinner table.

Regardless, your team is your team. And as a team, your successes are determined by your strongest links and limited by your weak links.

Healthy team relationships are critical to your emotional and physical wellbeing as well as to company success. Here I'm going to focus on the "how's" and "what's" which, when executed, result in healthy team relationships.

Learn and Adhere To My "5 Cornerstones of Ideal Team Members"

I'd like you to pause for a moment and reflect upon a time when you, yourself were not happy with a team member. I can guarantee you that the team member *lacked* one of the 'ideal' cornerstones below.

Starting tomorrow, do what you can to ensure *all* current and future team members possess the below qualities. The *rest* of your team will thank you profusely for your efforts!

Cornerstone 1: Competence

The ideal team member consistently demonstrates that they know what they are talking about, AND can back it up with performance and evidence. The 'competency' cornerstone is the bare minimum necessary criteria for a functional team member.

Cornerstone 2: Credibility

Team members can be competent, but not credible. Said differently, a beautiful resume without anyone validating or backing up their success isn't worth the paper it's written on. Your team members must be able to back up what they say by getting validation from your key stakeholders throughout the company. Without credibility, respect and trust from others is not a guarantee.

Cornerstone 3: Character

Character means having leadership acumen, morals, *and* an ethical compass. It means that you can be trusted to do the right thing – even when no one's looking, or when not everyone in the room wants to do the right thing.

Do your team members always try to do the right thing? Do they have a "pick up the trash on the floor when no one is looking" sort of persona? In most circumstances, having character surpasses competency and credibility.

Skills can be learned: it's more important that your team members can be trusted to do the right thing than that they know all the latest tools and techniques. Wouldn't you want every person on your team to have character?

To be clear, we are not looking for perfect *behavior*! We are looking for perfect *intent.*

The intent to be better than we were yesterday. The intent to try to converge, collaborate, support one another and win or lose…together.

Mistakes may be made due to lack of skill or knowledge – but the intent to do the best we can is consistent. That's character.

LIFE LESSON: Have humility and character and you will succeed. If you just have character and no humility, you will likely succeed, but you won't rest well. So do them both and make a difference in your life - and in the lives of others.

Cornerstone 4: Contribution

Team members at all levels, regardless of title, position or level of responsibility, are paid to perform. We are *all* expected to deliver on our promises and commitments to the company. The ideal employee understands this business contract and brings it every day to fulfill this contract.

Look for dedication, perseverance and a can-do attitude and you will find a team member dedicated to making a meaningful contribution and beyond.

Cornerstone 5: Culture Fit

Given my experience working with thousands of individuals spanning a multitude of diverse organizations and industries, I know that the number one factor that makes for an ideal team member is a 'cultural fit to the team.'

Your team member might have the competency, credibility, character, and contribution qualities, but if he is not a culture fit to the team, it's just *not* going to work.

This can be difficult to understand, because "team culture" can be difficult to understand. What are the components of a "culture?" These are things like unspoken habits, traditions, rules, expectations, conventions, beliefs, and agreements that your team all share.

You may not even notice that your culture is there until someone joins your team who doesn't fit into it. And then, you suddenly notice. This new person can perform the job description, and follow the written rules. But it becomes clear right away that they have different personal or professional attitudes, behaviors, and expectations than the rest of the team, or vice versa.

It might be a hard pill to swallow but believe me, count your losses now and move on. You will pay for it if you try to make it work.

Ensure Your Team is Always Aligned & Moving in the Same Direction!

One hundred percent of all team issues arise because there is a misalignment somewhere. It can be something as simple as a breakdown in communication about what is needed for project success, or as extreme as a full-blown workplace conflict. Either way, the result is frustration and lost productivity.

In my work, I have witnessed office shouting matches because a team has gotten *so* toxic. I have seen situations where team members were *intentionally* "back-stabbing" one another, or completely avoiding each other due to personal differences, while forgetting their shared goal.

In every case, the result was a toxic environment. It was an environment where, instead of productive, reliable, and harmonious work, conflict, lack of reliability, and inefficiency were expected.

Wharton management Professor Gregory Shea warns that: "leaders and teams can turn toxic through the misguided belief that being tough and unforgiving is a productive way to manage every employee."

In other words, this often happens when leaders don't feel that team members' relationships and emotional lives are worth addressing. Instead of aligning misaligned emotions, they simply bear down harder in their demands for productivity – often making personal resentments and lack of cooperation *worse* in the process.

Team "implosions" due to misalignment, regardless of the form they take, are situations that *must* be resolved *fast.* If they aren't, an entire company's strategy can be at risk.

What is the long-term effect of such a situation? The cost of a toxic environment is higher than we might believe. In INC Magazine, Professor Shea reports that workplace toxicity can range from physical abuse to feelings of anxiety and lack of safety that interfere with worker performance.[21]

Christine Porath, a Georgetown University professor of management, and Christine Pearson, professor at the Thunderbird School of Global Management at Arizona State University, have studied the impact of abusive and uncivil behavior among employees.

In a survey of 14,000 workers at all levels of corporate structure, Porath & Pearson found that nearly half of those who were subjected to uncivil behavior at work decreased their effort and intentionally

[21] Yakowicz, W. (2015, August 21). The True Cost of a Toxic Work Environment. Retrieved from https://www.inc.com/will-yakowicz/the-cost-of-toxic-environment.html?cid=search

spent less time at work, while 38 percent "intentionally decreased" the quality of their work.

A quarter of workers who experienced incivility from colleagues or supervisors reported taking their frustration out on their customers. Twelve percent ultimately left their jobs.

The cumulative loss from decreased effort, time, quality of work, and employee turnover was huge. In an article for Harvard Business Review, Porath & Pearson wrote: "Companies we've worked with calculate that the tab for incivility can run into the millions." Millions of dollars of revenue lost, due to failure to treat team members respectfully![22]

On the flip side, I've also been involved with teams that were completely aligned and moving in the same direction, with the same priorities and focus. Such teams always achieve amazing things.

I was once privileged to be part of a company that was looking at the potential of millions of dollars in losses for the next year, primarily due to the competitive impact of Amazon. If something wasn't drastically done to turn the company around, no one knew how bad the multiyear impact or the loss of fiscal revenue would be.

But the company was safe, because their team *was* ready to take drastic action, in the *right* direction.

Everyone laid their swords on the table. It wasn't about titles, which department was more important or even who was contributing the most to the bottom line.

It was about doing whatever had to be done to converge, align and become One Voice. One Voice on priorities, One Voice in mindset, One Voice in direction, One Voice in communication, and One Voice in Action.

What was the result? In the span of a few months, the team managed to turn the company from being in the red to having a net revenue of a few million dollars in the black

This feat was extremely challenging and painful. It required team

---

[22] Pearson, C. P. C. (2019, March 19). The Price of Incivility, Harvard Business Review. Retrieved from https://hbr.org/2013/01/the-price-of-incivility

members to adjust their expectations and make personal sacrifices. Yet it resulted in something extremely positive.

The reality: their company would have fallen to Amazon if they hadn't become One Team, with all eyes on the prize of success.

How can you achieve similar success with your team, regardless of where their alignment is right now?

Some Solid Ways to Align Your Team

1. **Align Mission, Vision Focus and Direction:** We spent ample time discussing these aspects in previous chapters. Your mission and vision are "the prize" you want to accomplish, and aligning your players toward these goals will help individual differences melt away.

2. **Align on Expectations:** Team members often get frustrated because they don't know what the leader's team expectations are, leaving them to disagree among themselves about how things should be done. Set clear expectations in terms of:

Communication

- What does the leader need to know/not know?
- What is the *best* form of communication to use among the team? Email, text, phone, face to face?
- How do the leader and your peers prefer the content/ information presented and reported? High level summary, detailed information, brief and to the point?
- Who communicates to the external and internal customers, and when?

Support Needs

- What does the team need *most* from the leader?
- What does the leader need *most* from the team?

Personal Value Needs

- How can the leader, *best* demonstrate that the team and its members are valued? How can they keep morale up by rewarding success?
- How can the team *best* demonstrate that the leader is valued?

- What values should we strive to embody and enact in our daily team lives – even if it means taking a few extra minutes or dollars each day?

Align on Roles and Responsibilities:

- Are we "as clear as a sunny day" on who does what, and owns what?
- Who is ultimately responsible for which outcomes and metrics?
- What's the difference between what the leader focuses on achieving on a daily basis, and what the team focuses on?

Example: During my work on one project, there had been multiple situations where there appeared to be a mutiny developing. The team members thought the leader spent time doing nothing, while they were working harder.

The problem was the leader's activities were not obvious. Since the team members did not see the leader doing crucial work, they assumed that nothing was being done by the leader.

The situation improved dramatically once the 'roles and responsibilities' for the team and leader were clearly laid out. In this case, those responsibilities looked like:

- Team: Responsible for day-to-day delivery of key responsibilities and expertise areas.
- Leader: Responsible for administration, coordination, prioritization, reports, back-fill, Team Voice, bridge to upper management.

Respect for the leader changed when responsibilities were clear. Once the team realized that the leader was not only doing something but, was completing tasks which the team had *no* interest in adding to their own to do lists, they realized that the leader's work was indispensable to the team's daily functioning.

Knowing clearly what people are responsible for and how the responsibilities contribute to the 'bottom line' and/or overarching goals of the company fosters a healthy sense of security and perceived value among team members.

This understanding is critical to taking care of your team.

Promote and Agree on Your Team Brand

It's easy for the whole team to get focused *internally* and lose sight of how your team is perceived by the whole company and external customers.

To assess the current state of your Team Brand, go to your stakeholders and ask them what their perception is of your Team Brand. For best results, ask for a brutally honest assessment – and be prepared to receive it well.

What would you do if your team received each of the following responses to that question?

- Your team is known across the company as a "high performing, collaborative" team.
- Your team is known as a "toxic, nobody wants to work with" team.
- Your team seems NOT to know how to get anything done!
- Your team is a team that *everyone* wants to be a part of!

Good news is good for the ego – but bad news is a tool you can use for improvement. What *first* step would you take, as a team leader, if you received negative feedback from others inside or outside of your company?

Why do you choose that as your first step?

Developing your Team Brand is a critical component to building the most optimal team relationships. Like your own, private mission and vision, it doesn't just improve your team's relationship with external entities: it also gives your team members a specific sense of meaning, and a reputation to strive to create for themselves.

The bottom line is you *have* to have a healthy team brand! It means *everything* in terms of having the respect and credibility you need to be heard throughout the organization.

Achieving your desired team brand requires intention and focus You must maintain a consistent high level brand perception across the company. This goal also gives team members a vision which is specific and important to their individual careers to align toward.

Take time to determine the following with your team:

- How do we want the team to be perceived across the company? (By the team members)
- What are the key characteristics we want the team to be known for throughout the company?
- How is the team currently being perceived?
- What do we need to do to close the gap between current perception and optimal perception?
- How do we make sure we are successfully meeting our Team Brand?

Make Time to Assess and Evaluate Team Performance

It's easy to get caught up in day-to-day business and "putting out fires," leaving no time for growth beyond your current capacities. Before you know it, the day, the week, the year is gone!

Don't fall into this trap. A healthy team takes time out *frequently* to assess Team Performance. This prevents the development of slow-growing, insidious problems, and allows the team's abilities to grow over time.

Imagine a professional sports team which continually assesses team performance on a game day, weekly, monthly, yearly and multi-year basis. Surely this team would show excellent results for individual players and its overall scoring alike!

Why wouldn't you do the same? For us, daily or weekly may be overkill. But waiting around for the big quarterly reviews won't cut it either! Scrambling to put out fires before your quarterly review does not yield long-term growth.

Here are three crucial areas which must *always* be continually assessed and measured on the Team Performance Front:

Area 1: Business Performance

What is our promise to the business? Have we fulfilled it?

- What did we set out to achieve this quarter?
- What are our KPI's (key performance indicators) that show whether we are winning or losing?
- What are we driving?

1. Efficiency gains?
2. Revenue gains?
3. Margin?
4. Are we spending time on reducing the costs of doing business, as well as working to increase the bottom line profit?

Area 2: Functional Performance

How strong/solid are our infrastructure/systems/processes to deliver on our promises?

- Are our core competencies fully leveraged and maximized?
- Are our processes up-to-date?
- Are our capabilities being fully leveraged?
- Where are we improving? Where are we still broken?

Area 3: Leadership Performance

Are our relationships and leadership healthy?

- Are we as leaders modeling ideal leadership behavior?

- Is there ownership and buy-in within the team towards our goals?
- Are we aligned within our team?
- Are we aligned with our stakeholders across the company?
- Is our Team Brand healthy?

The continual evaluation of team progress and performance is critical on many fronts. It keeps communication at peak efficiency. It keeps accountability at the forefront. It allows teams to pivot and be agile when necessary. It fosters transparency.

And most importantly, it fosters ownership and breeds the concept of "One Team."

This attitude, when embodied fully, can achieve things that a poorly-aligned team simply can't do.

Maximize Your Team's Talent

Maximizing team talent is not as easy as simply pushing the "That Was Easy" button. It's complicated. There are many different variables that impact team performance and maximum output.

Which talents are present will vary with each individual team, and which are needed will vary by project, industry, strategy, and more.

One thing is universal: the goal is always to have a team that is performing at its peak ability, where the individual talents are maximized and none are ignored.

Here are seven things you can start doing now to maximize your team's use of talent:

Trust Your Team

This sounds so cliché but many team leaders fall into the micromanaging trap and don't allow their team members any autonomy. This actually *limits* the team's performance to staying *only* within the team leader's personal capabilities.

You *must* get comfortable with allowing your team members to fail *small*. Without failure, there is no learning or growth. By giving team members autonomy and responsibility, you create a sense of empowerment and personal investment for each of them, and truly show that you trust them.

This will also give you the opportunity as team leader to overcome your fear of *not* being the smartest person in the room – a fear which has stifled countless great ideas because the team leader wanted to have the last word.

Invest in Your Team Financially, Emotionally, and Physically

Being on a team means treating people as *people* - not as interchangeable cogs in a machine. When you treat people like machines, you get autopilot, mechanical performance; when you treat them as people, you get dynamic, proactive, innovative performance.

You can improve your team's performance by...

Supporting Their Development Financially

Ensure you have a training and development budget. The need to constantly learn and grow is not going away.

Remember: your team's capabilities are only as good as their skills and training. Show that you care about your team's ongoing need to grow and develop by providing a budget for training and development.

So long as they can justify how their training helps enhance their role, allow them to make the choice on what they'd like to study. In this way you will end up with a more diverse, agile skill set than you would by permitting only assigned trainings.

Connecting with them Emotionally and Physically

According to Gallup, only 29% of employees are engaged at work. This means that 71% are disengaged! That's 71% of employees who are performing below their peak potential.[23] Want an engaged team? Connect with them! Know who they are on an emotional level. Figure out what motivates them. Tie their personal motivations to their work and they will maximize their engagement and output!

This also requires that you are physically present for them. Get out of your office, walk around, and connect to your people!

Put Your People in Their 'Superpower' Slot

Do you know the strengths and talents of each individual member of your team? It's not just about their skillsets and competencies, but also passions and people skills.

Great teams are the result of great individual players contributing to the common purpose in the way they are *best* at.

This may not always be limited to what appears on the books or on their resumes: many of the most irreplaceable 'superpowers' are those which aren't taught in schools or learned for career-driven purposes.

Make Sure Your Team Inputs Match Your Desired Outputs

What is your team's major contribution to its parent business? As the team leader, it is your responsibility to make sure your team is properly aligned to deliver on the business needs. How well is your team positioned to do this?

Make sure that all roles on your team are appropriate, relevant, and work interdependently to deliver on the major contributions expected of your team.

If you are putting the wrong goals and expectations into your team's meetings and strategies, you won't get the output you need!

Measure, Measure, Measure

---

[23] Rigoni, B., & Nelson, B. (2019, December 16). Few Millennials Are Engaged at Work. Retrieved from https://news.gallup.com/businessjournal/195209/few-millennials-engaged-work.aspx

You must have a way of determining whether or not you are getting the best out of your team. That's impossible without metrics.

What metrics you are using to measure your team's performance? Are these measured in terms of dollars, hours, production units, error rates, or scores on a satisfaction survey?

How often are you reviewing them with each individual member of your team to determine their own individual contribution?

Recognize, Reward and Hold Accountable

Recognize your team for their talents when appropriate. Showcase how they've used their strengths to deliver for the business.

At the same time, hold your team accountable when their work is just not good enough. Like a great head coach, you must push them to be better when their results and effort are not where they need to be.

Just remember: a high-performing organization improves its systems instead of blaming individuals when problems are widespread throughout the team. If multiple team members are having trouble performing, the problem may lie with the team leader, policy, resources, etc. rather than the individual team players.

Recognizing this isn't just fair to the players: it's better for the organization, which can't solve problems if it doesn't know their true cause.

Overcome Your "Inferiority Complex" if You Have One

Some team leaders have a fear of *not* being the smartest person in the room. They have an inferiority complex, and are afraid that other people's stellar performance might undermine their own.

What does this mean for their business? They don't hire anyone they think will be smarter than them!

I hope this is not you. It is impossible to have a fully leveraged team if you are a leader who has to

Some team leaders have a fear of *not* being the smartest person in the room. They have an inferiority complex be the smartest of the bunch. Fully max optimized teams have leaders in place who are fully dependent on their team members to own their areas of responsibility and contribute expertise.

The importance of your work relationships is no laughing matter. They will truly make or break you, as a professional and a performer! Individual contributors become managers because of their results as individual performers– not because of their likability. Yet managers often fail to grow in this role because they don't learn the skills of relationship management and optimization.

Once you become a team leader or manager, it's *not* about being the smartest person in the room, micromanaging your team, or ensuring that they "always perform as well as you do." It's about empowering and inspiring them to perform *better* than you do and contribute *better* ideas than you could contribute on your own.

Sometimes, this means stepping out of your comfort zone by allowing team members to try a new idea, make their own decisions about their training and schedule – and subsequently be personally accountable for the results. They might fail to meet their goals, or they might far exceed them when given such autonomy: you'll never know unless you let them try.

Without risk there is no reward and management is nothing if not the practice of maximizing the rewards a team is able to generate.

If you want to *win* at work, you *must* master the relationship side of working with teams and people. I hope the above gives you a good start.

Of course, the first person you lead is yourself. You are the one person you have the opportunity to lead and coach 24/7/365. And so your own abilities are a true measure of your leadership skills!

Now, let's take a moment to focus on optimizing *you,* and *your* emotional intelligence skills.

Chapter 13

Winning In Leadership & Emotional Intelligence

This entire book is based around the concept of 'thrival.' We've examined how to win in business and business relationships and in the pages to come we'll examine how to win and thrive in life and personal relationships as well.

One key skill is necessary to true "thrival." That is leadership. As individuals and businesspeople, our ability to accomplish anything depends on our ability to lead people and inspire them to accomplish all they can while working with us.

Leadership is your ability to consciously and observably impact others – and, most importantly, yourself. Just as our ability to achieve in business is limited by our leadership ability, so our ability to lead others is limited by our self-mastery.

This section will focus on you, yourself and what you can do better. We'll focus on a few dimensions I have not addressed at length in my previous book: "Many Parts, One Body: Healthier Leaders, Healthier Teams, a Healthier You."

Would others say you are a renter or an owner of your leadership space? Are you only doing the bare minimum to meet the leadership required to make it through the day or have you truly internalized your "call of duty" as a leader in business?

Leadership is about ownership. It's about having the guts to own what you do well and also own where you suck!

And believe me, we *all* have leadership areas where we suck. If you don't think you have any, it just means you haven't tested yourself to your limits yet. That's not a good thing!

Leadership is about ownership of yourself. It's about ownership of your actions, your words, your mindset and your life as a whole.

"Leadership" is a universal, unbiased term. It describes a behavior, *not* a privilege or a possession. Leadership is indifferent to title, power, authority or role.

True leaders are the ones who get things done. Period. We've probably all been in workplace situations where the person with the biggest title wasn't the person with the biggest results – but the one with the biggest results is the one that a smart business will promote and empower.

LIFE LESSON: Great leadership is about saying, thinking and doing *whatever* is needed to model the appropriate behavior for others. It's about empowering others. It's about continually striving to become our *highest* selves. It involves not only the actions we take, but also our words and thoughts.

Individuals with mediocre leadership skills have no idea how much negative impact they have on others. In fact, lack of understanding – and ownership – of the effects of one's actions on others is a trademark of a poor leader. Someone who consistently blames others for performance problems is surely dodging responsibility – or at least failing to pick it up – themselves.

Someone who feels they cannot impact others or cultivate themselves to the level that they can *positively* impact others is someone who hasn't yet learned what it takes to be a leader.

Remember, we are all parts of the same organization. Eventually, lackluster leadership in any department impacts *everyone* in the organization.

So let's not be the one who is unmindful about our impact on others. Let's be the one who leads by setting a great example, takes responsibility for their own actions, and knows how to motivate others.

Let's look at how we can truly become the very best leader we can be.

Besides being able to deliver on business results, strategy, and efficiencies, leadership is also about having the necessary level of emotional intelligence.

As we've discussed, people are the most important asset your business has. Our ability to motivate, inspire, and hold our people accountable determines our ability to get results.

In my experience, there are three critical areas where you *must* have emotional intelligence and leadership competencies. All are interrelated, interconnected and interdependent on one another.

The "Big Three" are:

1. **Mastery of Self**
2. **Understanding and Connecting with Others** (Review Relationships Section)
3. **Managing our Relationships** (Review Relationships Section)

We've now covered two of these – the two that involve other people.

It's time at last to cover the final, and perhaps most important component necessary for leadership: mastery of self.

Remember: emotional intelligence has *nothing to do with* your job title. It has to do with *you* and the impact that you have on *yourself and others.*

Mastery of Self

Many great books have been written throughout the ages on mastery of self. So how do we narrow this subject down into a simple to-do list? Here are the "big rocks" we can all use to develop our Mastery of Self:

- Awareness and Control
- Knowing – and Using – Your Superpower and Kryptonite

- The SAOL Leadership Ladder and Emotional Intelligence Matrix

We'll now go through these one by one, to explain how each tool can allow us to gain mastery of ourselves.

Awareness and Control

Many people balk when I discuss awareness. "What do you mean 'awareness,' Rubi? Of course I'm aware of everything I do, and of the effects of my actions!"

But the truth is, most of us are not aware of many of the things we do, or of the power we have in every given situation. Think of how often you go on 'autopilot,' or assume that something is just "obviously the way things are."

What if your "autopilot" could be improved? What if some of your "obvious facts" are not facts, but assumptions based on your own limited experience?

This is the stuff which sets masters apart from average and poor performers. Masters take measures to be truly aware and engaged, always examining their

> **'Mastery of Self' isultimatelyabout being as 'in control' as possible, despite what the environment, situation, circumstance or people throw your way.**

situation to determine how they could have done better. Mediocre and poor performers assume that "they've done all they can" or that "the outcome was out of their control."

Imagine having the ability to have the wherewithal to *always* be "the calm in the storm." Imagine being truly aware, in the moment, and fully present at all times. Imagine being able to *intentionally* make the determination of how you'd like to respond, react, communicate, take action, *before* you react or make a knee-jerk decision.

Imagine being able to pre-play countless interactions and scenarios that might occur at work, finding the best result through anticipation. It's as if you are Neo in The Matrix, seamlessly dodging each bullet that comes your way.

This becomes possible when you have a trained ability to slow everything down and be fully aware of what's going on *before* you respond.

These skills can be learned.

Mastery of self is about being as in control as possible, despite what the environment, situation, circumstance or people throw your way.

Think about this: how often have you reacted poorly or felt that you had "no choice" but to act in a way that resulted in impaired outcomes for everyone? How often have you looked back and *wished* you had been able to come up with a better outcome from a situation, but simply not seen any way that was possible in the moment?

This is the discipline of masters. Constantly learning what you *can* do better – and learning to "stop time before the bullet hits" so that you can take the ideal action in real time.

This is about being in emotional control, mental control, and in absolute control of how you will respond to *whatever* is going on.

Do you believe this is possible? It absolutely is! No one is able to accomplish this 100% of the time - but masters constantly strive to increase their success rates, and soon far exceed those who go through their days on "autopilot" or with the assumption that "I can't do any better."

So how do you cultivate these skills? The secrets are found in the martial arts – the real-world skills upon which Neo's mystical bullet-dodging abilities were modeled.

A Lesson From The Martial Arts

I practiced and taught Martial Arts from my early twenties through my late thirties. Chinese Kenpo, Grappling, Pentchak Silat, Weapons, Boxing, Kick-boxing, Point Fighting, and Katas. After my day job, I went to the martial arts schools where I taught and spent hours upon hours there with students.

I fought and taught with and against opponents of all sizes, strengths and capabilities. It was both a physical and a mental challenge for me. In order to be successful, I had to learn how to adjust to each opponent.

In fact, this is the true heart of martial arts: constantly testing and improving oneself through sparring matches, which force you to react in real-time.

When I first started sparring, I found myself reacting instead of responding to my opponents. This meant I simply mirrored what they gave me. I did not have the opportunity to consciously choose what my response would be. This limited me severely.

If they came at me hard, I came at them hard. If they wanted to grapple, I'd grapple. If they wanted to box, I'd box. Let me tell you, this often did not work out for me, especially if my opponent was a world class boxer or grappler. By reacting on "autopilot" instead of responding with conscious choice and strategy, I let my opponent determine my every move.

What I learned was that I had to adjust if I were to win. I had to develop the ability to stop myself and think strategically before responding to what my opponent threw at me.

I couldn't just box a boxer. I couldn't let my opponent choose the weapon for our match. Instead, I had to shift the course of events in a way my opponent was not expecting. I had to take him down to the ground where he was helpless.

I couldn't just grapple with a professional grappler. Instead, I had to do the opposite of what he was expecting: keep him upright for as long as possible, weaken him before taking him down.

I had to know what my strengths were and what they were not. I had to know what my opponents' strengths were and what they were not.

I had to adjust, and adjust quickly. I had to learn to truly be in the moment, aware, acting fast but thinking slowly.

How can we accomplish this outside of the sparring ring?

Knowing Who You Are

One way to ensure we respond strategically is to know our own strengths. I was able to outwit the master boxer only because I knew that he was better at boxing than I was. I was able to weaken the master grappler only because I knew that he was better at grappling than I was.

Society tends to pour on examples of who we *should be and who we shouldn't be*. We often spend more time thinking about who we think we *should* be than about who we *actually are*.

Society can even praise us for this: everyone should be the same, they say. We should all be good at everything.

But this kind of thinking is very dangerous for the simple reason that *we are not all the same*. No one is good at everything. And we all have some things we are *especially* good at. My opponents – the boxers and grapplers – knew what their strengths were. They knew what techniques they were better at than I was. They knew how to beat me.

In order to know their strengths, *they had to also know their weaknesses*. The boxer had to *know* that he was more likely to win boxing than grappling. The grappler had to *know* that he could beat me if he got me on the ground – but that he was not as good at fighting upright. Without knowledge of their weaknesses, these fighters would have been unable to leverage their strengths.

Without knowing who they were – the good, the bad, and the ugly – these fighters would not have been able to win. But through self-knowledge, they were able to become truly formidable forces. Not by becoming the impossible master of everything, but by leveraging their known strengths wherever possible, and avoiding or recruiting teammates to cover their areas of weakness.

Now imagine what would have happened if these fighters had needed to believe they were good at everything. Imagine what would have happened if they denied having any

> **Many people claim they know who they are, but few can claim they are the 'Master of themselves.'**

weaknesses. They wouldn't have been nearly so formidable, would they? They would not have been able to strategize effectively to beat me.

So how do we know who *we* are? How do we find our unique strengths and weaknesses, in order to become the strongest possible winning machine? How do we find the ways in which we are meant to be *unique* from everyone else, and turn those to our advantage?

Mastering ourselves starts with re-discovering ourselves.

This might sound paradoxical to some, who imagine that "self-mastery" means being good at everything. It does not. Any military strategist will tell you that anyone who says they're equally good at everything is either deluding themselves, or has failed to excel at *anything*.

Instead, self-mastery begins with knowing ourselves honestly, warts and all. Who are we really when all of the covers are pulled off? Who are we at our core compared to the surface level?

My observation: Many people claim they know who they are, but few can claim they are the "master of themselves."

Self-mastery, like all great arts, means mastering a balance of opposites. In this case the opposites are radical self-acceptance, and radical self-improvement.

I challenge you to take a step back and take a look in the mirror. Take a moment, an hour, or a day of silence to go within and ask yourself the questions on this checklist.

I challenge you to *write down the answers to these questions* as you ask them. You might be surprised by what comes out of your own fingers!

- ❑ Where do you believe you are *better* than anyone in the world?
- ❑ What really motivates you?
- ❑ What are you really passionate about? Why?
- ❑ What are your natural talents?
- ❑ What type of people do you like to be around?

- ❑ What type of people drive you crazy?
- ❑ What are your pet peeves or triggers that set you off?
- ❑ Where do you find yourself often beating yourself up critically?
- ❑ What expertise do you have?
- ❑ What do you want to be your legacy at the end of the day?
- ❑ What's most important to you?
- ❑ How would you describe your highest self?

Remember: this is about you, and you alone. You, and you alone, are your most powerful tool.

Your own capabilities and motivations – honest knowledge of them – are the most powerful tool you can leverage toward personal and professional goals.

Ultimately, you'll start to see all of these questions are interrelated to one another, and all revolve around your Superpower!

Chapter 14

Discover Your Superpower

Let me ask you to pause for a moment and reflect on this one, *very* important question: **What do you believe you are *naturally better at* than anyone in this world?**

This can be anything. It doesn't have to be a traditional "job skill." Think about social skills, hobbies, passions, etc.. As this chapter progresses, you may be surprised to find just how applicable this skill can be to your job and your business goals!

In a word, *that thing which you are best at is* your superpower.

Later, I'll ask you some more questions to help you pinpoint what this might be. But before we do that, I want *your* answer. I want you to have this in your mind as we move forward.

Remember, I am asking *what you are best at.* That means it doesn't matter how good you think you are at things compared to other people. We are only comparing *your own skills* to each other.

If you truly can't decide which of a few skills you have are strongest, then *which one do you love doing more?*

Truth: Embracing and harnessing your Superpower will set you free more than you might believe is possible!

Our Superpowers help us to overcome weaknesses and obstacles. When harnessed properly, they also allow us to deliver performance no one else is capable of in almost any field.

Believe it or not, our failure to leverage this Superpower – no matter how oddly specific it may seem, such as if you said "playing video games" or "swing dancing" - is at the heart of all of our failures and frustrations. For hidden within this Superpower is the unique skills and capacities which will cause you to excel at business.

All of us want to feel validated, valued, and connected as people. In fact, human connection is so important that warm social contact and a sense of belonging have been linked to longer life and lower mortality rates.

What does this have to do with our Superpower and its use in business? Quite simply, a properly used Superpower can be used to accomplish that validation, value, and connection.

Our Superpower is an integral part of who we are. It is also something that can amaze, provide value, and ultimately provide a need for our presence and a place where we absolutely feel we belong when we leverage it properly.

Using Our Superpower is how we receive value and validation from others.

Now, you may still be wondering how to use your Superpower in business. Very often, the thing we are absolutely the best at is something we don't immediately recognize as a business skill. That's because these skills and their underpinnings often begin to develop at a very young age. They are a very basic part of who we are, far pre-dating our career plans or job description.

But our nature is smart. It doesn't teach us things that are useless. Even if it has never occurred to us to bring our empathic ability, or swing dancing expertise, or strategy game skill to the board room, we have probably all been surprised by how useful these skills can be in daily life.

How often has your empathetic nature helped your team perform better, even if this didn't result in a pay raise? How readily does your love of swing dancing translate into bringing rhythm and exhilaration to customer relations or team dynamics? How much better might you perform in business if you conceptualized your company like it was your Star-craft clan?

To give you a more detailed example, let's look at *my* superpower. This superpower developed at home, outside of the business world - but it has allowed me to succeed both in the corporate world, and in building my own consulting firm.

My Superpower And Where It Came From

Those of you who have read my previous book, "Confronting My Elephants," know that I had a fairly intense childhood. After losing my father and being smuggled out of Vietnam during the Vietnam War, I was orphaned when my mother was killed by a drunk driver in our new hometown in the United States.

My siblings and I were allowed by the courts to remain together and raise each other – which often left us penniless, in addition to being targeted for discrimination. We were often surrounded by people who were angry about losing loved ones in the still-ongoing Vietnam War, and who did not fully understand that we were on their side of the conflict.

Being left in a hostile environment with very few resources and very little support led to the creation of my superpower.

As heart wrenching as my life experience was, it made me "The Resolution Driver."

From a very early age, I had to learn to solve *any* problem using few to no resources. I had to find a way to find or *make* resources where no obvious ones appeared. I had to learn to resolve personal differences and obtain cooperation from practically anybody, no matter how prejudiced or stubborn they might have started out.

My Superpower has been with me ever since childhood! There is no problem too big for me, nor any situation too desperate. This continues to be the way I approach life and the way I serve others.

At my Fortune 100 employer, I used this approach of constant problem-solving and resource creation to get noticed and quickly work my way up the corporate ladder. In my consultancy I use my Superpower to quickly determine what needs to be done, regardless of the problem, and help them 'connect and drive resolution.'

So what *is* your Superpower?

What do you do *better than anyone else?*

Now, the leap that is a challenge for many people: *how can these same skills apply to your career?* How can you use what you do best to get noticed, get paid, and become valued as a uniquely skilled individual?

Superpowers are real, and we all have them! Whether consciously or unconsciously, we are all actively using our Superpowers *every day* to bring validation and value to our lives!

Yet we may sometimes think of our Superpower as something which "only applies outside of work," or "can't be used in our job description."

If that really is true, it may be time to look for a new job description! Our precious Superpowers bring us both high performance and high satisfaction when leveraged properly.

It is critically important, especially in leadership, to learn how to maximize our Superpower *and* make sure it doesn't get out of control/

What do I mean by your Superpower "getting out of control?" We'll discuss that in a few moments.

For now, let's look at some examples of superpowers I've discovered in my coaching and consulting clients:

Actual Superpowers from Clients

Superpower	Where it Came From	How It's Leveraged at Work
The Connection and Resolution Driver	Need to belong and fit in and be good enough.	Driving resolutions pertaining to Organizational leadership and strategy, creating value for me and the organization.
The Artful Converger	Always had to integrate the dichotomy of family interests between mother and father.	Strategic integration and planning at the highest levels.
The Unique Maximizer	How to stand out and be recognized growing up.	Optimizes university student development and leadership.
Visionary Inclusionator	Always sought to represent the under-represented.	Taking company and people to higher heights and new frontiers.
Succinctly Dependable	Had to be the dependable one for her family growing up.	Interdepartmental champion and "right hand" to CEO
The All Angles Appeaser	Had to become the family "center"	Human Resource and Capital Integrator of his company.
Infectious Encourager	Chose to be positive light in the midst of the chaos.	Board President and primary influencer of congregation "buy-in" and support

To Shine Logically	Grew up very poor and figured out a way to stand out, rise above and shine.	Product to Consumer Innovator and 'Translator' of what works/doesn't for the Consumer

Created by Rubi Ho

What's Your Superpower?

Don't rush this process. Address the following questions and actions steps. Perfection is not the goal here, just get close for starters.

Where do You Believe You are Naturally Better than Anyone Else?

Take a moment to reflect on what has come easily for you all of your life. This is the single biggest indicator to what your superpower might be. Consider your Superpower as a "God-Seed," or "Gift," given to you for a purpose so that you are able to cope with life's inevitable challenges.

Reflect deeply here. Don't rush it. Go back as far as you can remember, and see if you can uncover what you've done to bring value to yourself. Think of it as your positive thread, your "contribution" to every situation in your life.

What have you often been able to do better than other people? What have people asked you to do for them, because you were better at those things than they were themselves? What recurring positive comments have people, especially those who know you well, made to you or to others about you?

Maybe you believed those positive comments. Maybe you didn't. Write them down anyway. Remember, humility is not thinking less of yourself, but thinking of yourself less often!

What are you discovering in this process? You'll know you are close to the answer when things start to make sense and you start to see patterns.

Ask Others Who Know You Well What They Believe Your Superpower Is

Simply reach out to them, describe the idea of a "Superpower" and then ask them: *"If I were to have a Superpower, what do you think it would be? What makes you say that?"*

A word of caution here. A wise person once observed that "Every conversation is a conversation with ourselves."

Rather than saying "Oh, they just don't really know me," change the response in your head to "Wow! That is so true. How did I miss that? What can I do with this new insight into myself?'"

Use Assessment Tools

Many assessment tools such as Strengthsfinders, DiSC or 'the Birkman have been created to help people discover their strengths and weaknesses. These won't tell you *exactly* what your superpower is, but they will point you in the right direction.

Your Superpower will be more specific than the answers provided by these tests – but these tests can help you clarify the right ballpark to look in, and help you see what you do *not* enjoy doing. You'll need the answers to the questions we've discussed above in order to help crystallize what your Superpower might be.

Take all of this information and ponder it for a few days. Look at the answers you've gotten from loved ones, colleagues, and memories of what people have told you over the years.

Write up a summary of what you feel are your Superpower strengths and run it past co-workers, friends, relatives and anyone else you trust. They may agree with you, question your assessments, or point out some strength you had totally missed in yourself. Take their feedback and further refine.

Once you have identified your Superpower, determine how to leverage it more fully in your work and your life.

This can mean setting up goals at work which you can be recognized for as a top performer – and which can be accomplished using your Superpower. It may mean adding activities to your personal life which will allow your Superpower to shine and create value for those you love at home.

This may require a conversation with your boss, or your spouse. It may require some strategizing as to how to be recognized or rewarded for using your Superpower in the workplace.

Take this leap and you WILL find that your life, including your work, is more rewarding!

Now, Go Save the World!

With the use of our superpower, we are moving towards becoming our highest self. This is someone who is definitely, uniquely *you* – someone who is the best you it is possible to be.

In this "highest-self zone," the goal is to find a work role that allows you to maximize your Superpower.

Don't be surprised if you find your current work setting a mismatch and that you are under-leveraged. This is very common, since career decisions and job descriptions often don't take into account rare and priceless "soft skills," such as social and strategy skills.

Don't panic if you find yourself in this situation!

With your newfound understanding of who you really are and how to maximize your talents, create a strategic plan for yourself. Slowly but methodically, do what you need to do to position yourself in the workplace so that you can fully leverage your Superpower.

This may mean pursuing a new job title, a new employer, or creating a new program or position right where you are which allows you to make maximum use of your unique skill.

At first it may feel "ambitious" or "demanding" to suggest changes around your workplace – but if it allows you to leverage your Superpower to the greatest possible benefit for your company, they will thank you for it!

Our Superpowers, When Overused, Become Our Kryptonite

Ok, now for the 'other side of the coin.' It's always possible to have too much of a good thing. Every virtue, in excess, becomes a vice. And every strength, in excess, becomes a weakness.

Even Superman and Captain America would be an annoyance in our lives if we didn't have any problems that needed saving. They would feel like a wet blanket as they hovered around us, because we wouldn't really need them to help us. We would just be annoyed at this very righteous person watching over us, acting like we couldn't do things for ourselves.

Believe it or not, your Superpower, if overused, can feel the same way to others.

Believe me, I'm speaking from personal experience! I can't tell you how often my wife has had to tell me: "I don't need you to resolve my problem! I just need you to listen to me!" Get the picture?

As critically important as it is for us to leverage our Superpower, it is *just* as critical for us to be able to constrain it so it does not become Kryptonite for our work and personal relationships.

But here's the good news: *Mastery of your Superpower results in your ability to overcome almost 100% of your emotional intelligence weaknesses!*

Why? As stated earlier, we as humans, have a never-ending desire to be validated and valued. How do we do this? You guessed it, by using our Superpower!

Pay attention to the times when you become irritated with others, or when they become irritated or hostile with us. You will likely soon find that at the root of *most* of these incidents is your Superpower. Either you are irritated with not being allowed to use it, or someone else is irritated that you are *trying* to. We can think of these as times when our Superpower is "fighting" with those around us.

Want to see me upset? Interfere with my ability to drive resolutions!

Want to see my wife shut-down? Dampen her ability to shine by trying to solve all her problems for her.

Would you like to see a CEO blow his top? Cut off his ability to be relevant.

As we observe these patterns, we can decide: is this a battle we want to "win," or do we want to avoid a battle altogether by refusing to fight?

Like the martial arts strategist on the sparring mat, we can ask: what approach will yield the best outcome? Will everyone be happier if I engage in the fight, or if I smile and graciously make way for others?

Like any hero's Superpower, ours can be used for good or evil. We can use it when the world really needs saving – or we can use it to dominate those around us and restrict their freedom.

So as you discover your very powerful abilities, be sure that you use them *responsibly*. You can save the world when it comes to company strategy. But perhaps you don't want to interfere in the lives of your family members and colleagues, unless they have asked you to!

Our Kryptonite rears its head each and every time our Superpowers are repressed.

We maximize our emotional intelligence when we can control our Superpower and decide: is my power really needed here? Has someone asked me for help?

Let's look at how we can manage the "wet blanket" side of our Superpower.

Managing Our Kryptonite

My personal Kryptonite, as the 'Resolution Driver' is that I can be extremely dismissive of people who *don't* resolve their problems. I can also resolve *other people's* problems without seeking permission! At times, this can make me a bit like Superman in a dystopian world: he is so convinced he knows what's best for everyone that he can become an oppressor!

In addition, I can push for closure when others are not ready. Because I have been forced to *act quickly* in my life, I don't always recognize when people need *time* or *space* to process their emotions. This results in me shutting down because my help has been rejected – or intimidating others, which is definitely not what I want to do!

All superheroes – yourself included – can face similar problems. We must be consciously vigilant to see if we are using our Superpowers in a way that does not respect other people, or in a way that does more harm than good!

In understanding our Kryptonite, it is important to be able to identify *when* we are experiencing a Kryptonite effect, and to know what to do when this happens.

Let's look at some Superpower examples, the benefits and what happens when they *aren't* appreciated (the triggers), resulting in the Kryptonite effect.

Superpower	When Appreciated	Kryptonite Effect	Trigger
The Resolution Driver	Appreciated for resolving people and organizational issues.	Can be dismissive Can get into resolving other's problems without permission	1) People don't want my help in resolving their problem 2) People aren't solving their own problem
The Artful Converger	Appreciated for creating master strategy decks and visuals showing how everything fits together.	Will "hoard" information until it's "artful," giving off the impression of being secretive and not inclusive	Afraid of looking stupid so won't show information till it's 'perfect'
The Unique Maximizer	Appreciated for maximizing student's potential.	Difficult to admit faults and ask for help	Afraid of looking inferior so won't share anything unless it's "unique"

Visionary Inclusionator	Appreciated for setting the vision for the company and involving everyone	Can be non-confrontational and delay accountability Can exclude people	1) Fear of alienating someone 2) Work is not being appreciated for being 'visionary'
The All Angles Appeaser	Appreciated for being empathetic and understanding others	Can become extremely indecisive	Too many people to please at once
Infectious Encourager	Appreciated for being the encourager of the group and attitude	Can be overly emotional and extreme and even shut down completely	No one is responding to the "infectious encouraging"
To Shine Logically	Appreciated for quality of work and output	Can shut down when work is not recognized and even become aggressive	Work is not being appreciated and showcased

Created by Rubi Ho

Truth: You will never become your highest self if you can't manage your Kryptonite.

When you have identified your Superpower, it becomes easy to be powerful. It is less easy to be both powerful *and* good.

Everything outside of your Superpower is *secondary* when it comes to improving your emotional intelligence. It is this thing that you are best at that will point the way to your social strengths *and* weaknesses. I feel strongly about this because I've seen it play out time and time again.

This is because your Superpower is closely associated with your "why." The same factors which form your Superpower also form your most powerful motivations and habits in life.

Spend the quality time needed to master understanding of your

Superpower – and any Kryptonite habits that might come with it - and you will be well on your way to achieving your 'highest self!'

Write answers in the chart below to help you get started managing your Superpower:

What is Your Superpower?	When Is It Appreciated?	What are your Kryptonite Weaknesses?	What Sets off your Weaknesses? (Trigger)
Example: The Resolution Driver	Appreciated for resolving people and organizational issues.	Can be dismissive Can get into resolving other's problems without permission	People don't need a problem resolved People aren't solving their own problem

Created by Rubi Ho

Working on Your Kryptonite: This Work Never Ends, But It's Worth It!

You are *never* going to completely eliminate your weaknesses! If that were possible, we wouldn't have people working for decades or whole lifetimes to become masters of their skill or industry, would we?

But you can *always get better.*

The goal of this work is simply to prevent your weaknesses from over-shadowing your strengths. It is to always remain the hero – never the villain.

To make this practical for you, I'd like you to make an inventory of the *most* important people in your life. If you are cultivating both business and personal goals, you may wish to include a few figures from both your work and your family or personal life.

It's with *these* people that managing your Kryptonite matters most. Everyone else is secondary. Make it a goal to *not* butt heads or be the "wet blanket" to the *most* important people in your life.

Make it your goal to ensure your Superpower always supports them – but never frustrates them or makes their lives more difficult.

For most, it's going to be *all* of the folks in the "relationships" sections of this book. Try answering these questions below to make sure you get your most complete answer:

- ❑ Who are the people in your life that will receive benefit from you working on yourself?
- ❑ What can you start doing to ensure only your Superpower is being felt, and *not* your Kryptonite?
- ❑ How will you know if you are being a "wet blanket" on others?
- ❑ What will you do differently if you realize this is happening?
- ❑ Who will you tell that you are working on being better?

On the flip side, what can you do to better leverage the Superpowers of others?

This might seem like a tall order. After all, we can't determine what other people do. But we *can* make them aware of what we think their Superpowers are. And if we see opportunities to use these for the greater good or for their *own* greater good, we can show them these opportunities.

The people around you are already showing you their Superpowers, simply by being themselves. Watch their words, their actions, how they interact with you, what matters to them, and you'll have the clues you need to see how they would like to be appreciated.

Even better, take them through the same set of actions that you've been exposed to in this book and find out directly!

Can you imagine a work environment where everyone feels truly appreciated and leveraged? The sky is the limit in this type of work setting – both for personal satisfaction, and for the value the team creates for others!

Chapter 15

The SAOL Leadership Ladder

I don't know how high you want to climb the ranks of corporate America. Do you want to be a CEO? Or just pay your bills with a nice amount left over for retirement savings and investing?

That's not up to me – so I'll give you the very best advice I can to help you shoot for the top to maximize your opportunities and value.

At the very least, I'd like to leave you with the SAOL Leadership ladder in case you decide to shoot for a high level executive position.

What is a "Leadership Ladder?" These are tools which aim to help people develop the skills they need to progress steadily up the corporate ladder, all the way to the C-suite. They are designed to teach skills that can be used to run a big corporation, or your own small business or volunteer organization, depending on your desire. Many different versions of the "Leadership Ladder" tool exist.

John Maxwell's "5 Levels of Leadership" is a great one that I highly recommend becoming familiar with. It stems from the "Servant Leader" angle we've discussed earlier in this book, and is very powerful. [24]

The "SAOL (Strategic, Agile, Organizational, Leadership) Leadership Ladder" is my own version of a Leadership Ladder. I created it to fill in gaps I encountered when using existing tools with my clients and mentees. Its focus is on developing business skills and a "company steward" mindset, in addition to the "Servant Leadership" mindset.

---

[24] https://www.skillsoft.com/resources/john-maxwell-the-5-levels-of-leadership/

For best results, you need *both* servant leader skills *and* SAOL business leadership skills to move up the corporate ladder. No matter how much respect you have from other people, lack of business leadership skills will stunt you when you are asked to produce results for an organization.

Conversely, great business leadership skill without a servant leader mindset may result in a high degree of competence – but no followers or supporters!

In many situations, the best and brightest of employees are promoted to management positions based on *technical skills* instead of *people skills.* This means that many people can flounder once promoted, negatively impacting themselves, their staff and the company.

This creates a sort of catch-22: in many cases, you cannot gain all of the skills needed for a high-level position *until you are in that high-level position.*

The challenge in every organization is to candidly assess every leader and have a clear plan to advance their development. This means allowing for on-the-job learning while minimizing damage from mistakes, and keeping an eye out for people who seem to already possess the most difficult skills.

The challenge for every leader is to do the same for themselves. We'll discuss here which skills you may wish to start cultivating to help you get into a position where they'll be needed.

Where Do You Rank Today?

The SAOL "Leadership Ladder" succinctly captures the primary contribution of leaders at each level. Which one of these ladder rungs describes you best?

The SAOL Ladder		
Peak Level	**Company Steward** • Demonstrates a Company-First mindset • Wholistic leadership approach integrating culture, profitability, overall company performance AND Organizational Health • Embraces the highest levels of company stewardship and accountability	**Target for Highest Potential Leaders to Reach this Level The Ideal C-Suite Leader**
Level 4	**Developer of Others** • Focused on growing talent and a strong leadership bench • Serves as a "head coach" versus "field player" • Models company values, leadership, culture	**Most Desirable Leadership Model for Majority of Company Leaders**
Level 3	**Effective Company Contributor and Integrator** • Consistently contributes to company bottom line and/or efficiencies • Contributes BEYOND own function and seeks ways to partner ACROSS the organization • Breaks down company silos	**The Level where MOST Level 1 and 2 leaders fall short of "breaking through"**
Level 2	**Strong Functional Leader & Team Builder** • Effectively ensures delivery of expectations within function owned • Empowers team to perform at higher levels	**Majority of <u>Every</u> Organization's Leaders Reside in the 2 Lowest Leadership Levels**
Level 1	**Leadership-Based Title and Functional Competency** • Holds influence over staff due to positional authority • Executional and tactical excellence	

Created by Rubi Ho

Level 1: Leadership Based on Title and Functional Competency

This level is very similar to John Maxwell's "5 Levels of Leadership.

At this level, a leader is great at executing strategies and reaching goals. But the task is more "following a script" while acting as a self-leader and role model to others. This level leader is more managing than coaching.

Level 2: Strong Functional Leader and Team Builder

A strong functional leader is one who has a *very* good grasp on what matters most in their function. This leader can keep on top of performance and constantly seek ways to keep the function efficient, reliable and dependable.

Most companies have the majority of their leaders at this level *so long as there are a few who have moved onto the higher levels!* Most companies only have a small number of Level 3-5 leaders. And often the peak leaders in terms of performance aren't even at the top in terms of job title!

With respect to team, a level 2 leader earns the respect and trust of their subordinates. This is done by:

1. Helping them focus on results
2. Ensuring clarity in expectations
3. Providing ongoing support and communication
4. Holding them accountable for their performance
5. Not getting in the way of his team's growth

Level 3: Effective Company Contributor and Integrator

This is what I call the "ceiling" level that *must* be broken through. Most leaders *do not break through*, and so do not go on to take the next step in their careers!

At Level 2, we spend so much of our time taking care of our

function, we get obsessed with it. Like Smeagol in Lord of the Rings, we lose sight of the world beyond our specific function. Our function becomes our "precious," and we hold onto it like it's the most important thing in the world!

This, unfortunately, prevents our own growth in the wider world. It can even cause us to come across as uncooperative or counterproductive to others.

You know you have fallen into this Smeagol role if over 90% of your work time is spent in the "day to day" business of putting out fires related to your role.

At this level it is always difficult to put in the extra effort needed to become a leader who can move to the next level – but this difficulty makes it all the more necessary to advance.

Helping leaders break through to Level 3 is where I spend most of my time as a coach and consultant! Training Level 3 leaders is necessary to create organization-wide change, because it is only this type of leader who is able to take the proactive, strategic, agile approach that is needed for drastic business success.

What separates a Level 3 leader from a Level 2 leader? It is an overriding "What is best for the company?" mindset which includes, but also transcends the "What is best for my function?" mindset.

Level 3 leaders ask:

1. What are the primary company priorities, and how do my function's priorities and my business partner's priorities compliment or accomplish the company priorities?
2. How do my function and my team support the company stakeholders?
3. How do I compliment what my interdepartmental partners are working on, instead of competing with or disregarding them?

4. How do we as a company work together to be more efficient, aligned, convergent, and productive?

Leaders can display fairly low emotional intelligence at Levels 1 and 2 and still perform in their job functions. Not so with Level 3! To get results, this level requires:

1. **Tremendous discipline.** Sometimes it's necessary to "sacrifice" and "take one for the team" if your own priorities are secondary to the good of the organization.
2. **Relationship skills.** This is about learning how to compromise, get along, be respected and have strong communication skills when working outside of your function. People who are unable to compromise intelligently will not be able to function at this level.
3. **Capacity to negotiate.** This means being reasonable and seeking to understand what is important and valid about contrary viewpoints. It is about getting to the best solution, not about "being right." This requires listening and empathy as well as strategic big-picture thinking.
4. **Emotional mastery.** This means managing your emotions when you are upset about something, and just importantly, calming the emotions of your colleagues and direct reports if *they* are upset! This is what really sets a great leader apart: the ability to manage the emotions in a room in ways that lead to long-term cooperation. If you can do this, you can make things happen. This allows us to identify potentially isolated silos and keep people focused on being One Team when things get personal or strong differences of opinion emerge.
5. A Level 3 leader has to operate at the highest levels of emotional intelligence in order to do what is needed to converge the various elements and people under her command. This is critical for healthy relationships. This is critical for progress. This is critical for productivity and meeting organizational goals.

In addition, Level 3 leaders help the team to break down silos while encouraging partnerships across the waters and between departments.

Level 3 leaders do this by:

1. **Focusing on communication.** These Level 3 leaders keep team members informed by sharing what's going on *beyond* their team. They do this with their priorities, words, and actions. They are always clear in communicating:
   a. What matters to the company
   b. What matters to other functions
   c. What matters to the team itself

Good communication of relevant information results in clarity, which results in good decision making!

2. **Providing Support. Level 3 leaders support, and are sometimes present for, team member cross-functional interactions.**

   Sometimes team members need back-up in cross-functional meetings. Remember, we all carry this Smeagol trait that makes it difficult at times to listen to others – or be heard by them. Having a Level 3 leader present for important cross-functional meetings helps add perspective and can reduce the chances of peer conflict and needless disagreement.

3. **Being a Partner. Level 3 leaders foster healthy partnerships across functions!**

   The *best* way to help our team members to have healthy cross-functional partnerships is for *us* to have healthy cross-functional partnerships. If we as team leader fail to model the behavior we are asking of our team, we are not doing anyone any favors.

In fact, we may well be missing benefits to our own function, or failing to diffuse tensions at the leadership level, by failing to engage in these cross-functional partnerships ourselves.

Level 4: Developer of Others

At this level of leadership, our most crucial task is working on *replacing ourselves*.

Did you get that? At this level, we are working on becoming extinct, becoming irrelevant, at least in our current role!

This allows us to move on to other roles – and to become known as a producer of excellent leaders in our field.

Level 4 leaders have the maturity and discipline to let go and move on! This is especially challenging because all of our "what if" anxieties come into play here:

- What if I don't have another job after I replace myself?
- What if the person I find to replace me looks, acts and performs better than me?
- What if I don't know what to do with myself once I replace my position?
- What if I don't know how to perform at the next level?

This work is so difficult – and so valuable – *because* it is so scary. Great leaders who can reproduce themselves become sources of infinite value. Yet they can only do this by facing and overcoming every fear we commonly acquire on our way up the corporate ladder. Most leaders fail to do this.

These fears are non-productive, and indeed counter-productive, for highly developed leaders. We develop our people, and by developing others we move ourselves in a position to move up the ladder. Yet the fear of losing our place is still very real!

At this level, the leader's ability to grow *becomes tied to their company's ability to grow*. Level 4 leaders may find themselves in need of a higher-level organization if their organization is not eager and prepared to give work to an ever-growing supply of Level 4 leaders.

Put simply, there is no way an organization can grow if it is not growing its talent! The amount of value a company can provide is limited by its number and caliber of leaders, so a Level 4 leader who produces more Level 4 leaders should be welcome and highly valued.

However, some Level 4 leaders do find themselves in a position where their company does not know how, or is not willing, to provide places for more high-level leaders.

The good news is, this means you have outgrown your company! It is time to move on to a company that does have its growth priorities in line.

In just the same way that companies can only grow if they are willing to delegate work to more leaders, *we ourselves* cannot grow if we are not willing to train others to replace us, and then delegate work to them.

At both the individual and organizational level, our capacity to create value now depends not on our own individual skills, but on our ability to *find or create other skilled leaders* so that the value we provide grows far beyond our individual abilities to create value alone.

Here's a very brief, high-level overview of how Level 4 leadership can best be leveraged to grow both your own career, and your company:

Focus on Growing Talent and Leadership: Create a Strong "Bench"

A Level 4 leader needs to have a "Number 2." This is the person who is second in command. This is one great way of distinguishing a Level 4 leader from earlier levels: most leaders don't have a Number 2 in place, or even identified for training!

Why? Most often, it is a fear of being replaced, or becoming irrelevant. Most leaders who have not recognized their full capacity "need to feel needed" - they are afraid that if anyone else becomes *too* good at their job, their own perks and position may be threatened.

However, as we've seen, the power of a leader who makes themselves indispensable in their current job pales in comparison to the power of a leader who produces *more* leaders. Being indispensable in your current role is a great way to ensure you are never promoted to a higher level!

So how do you choose your successor?

Here's a surprise: you may wish to let others make this choice! Training a new leader requires buy-in from the whole team. You will accomplish the conditions for great leadership training most easily when other stakeholders get a say in the decision of who becomes your Number 2.

Some refer to this as the "successor's dilemma." It can be difficult to get buy-in or agreement on who will take over a department or company when you're gone, and if buy-in isn't achieved your designated successor will have trouble gaining skills and respect.

A past article in the Harvard Business Review gives us an idea about how big a deal it is:

"The successor's dilemma presents a pair of damning alternatives. If a CEO resists passing the torch, his would-be successor can wage open war to win the top job—but that can get ugly and rarely works. Or the successor can resign—a "solution" that can seriously damage the successor's reputation and his wallet. He may walk away relatively unscathed, but a high-profile failure might make second chances hard to come by.

"The successor's dilemma is exacerbated by the fact that few people in an organization can help the successor and the CEO work out their crisis. Most boards of directors drop out of sight once the successor is hired; they check in only periodically. Similarly, most human resources executives don't play a mitigating role, primarily because few of them are the kind of trusted advisers necessary to negotiate a peace treaty between the CEO and his designated successor. Thus the CEO and his would-be heir are on their own to overcome, or be overcome by, the successor's dilemma. It's the latter that happens most often."[25]

So how do you avoid being beaten by this tricky situation?

Steps To Prepare For Letting Go

We've all heard the phrase "Rome wasn't built in a day." All great things take time to achieve if they are to be done properly. This definitely applies to letting go and replacing yourself as a leader. It took years for you to achieve the level of skill and responsibility you have; don't expect your successor to learn it all overnight.

Instead, determine the things that you can start to let go of and give those initial, smaller, safer responsibilities to your potential successor.

This provides a safety net for everyone involved. You are still available to right your ship if something doesn't go according to plan; your successor has the opportunity to learn on the job without being overwhelmed or risking catastrophic failure; and you can be assured that your ship is in good hands when the time comes to step aside entirely.

This builds confidence and creates empowerment for everyone involved. We are providing a growth opportunity for ourselves, our successor, and our organization. At the same time, we get to gradually focus our attention and time on other things. We are also spared the enormous "all or nothing" shift from one position immediately into a new position or task.

Continue to add to your successor's responsibilities as performance is demonstrated, and provide new opportunities as they grow.

Think About the Next Level Now!

Whether your "next step" is retiring or moving up the corporate ladder, it's wise to focus on how you'll get there *now*. Our next step

---

[25] Watkins, D. C. M. D. (2014, August 1). The Successor's Dilemma. Retrieved from https://hbr.org/1999/11/the-successors-dilemma

is always the most important step that's available to us, our doorway to new opportunities.

The irony is that *most* leaders do not plan for the next level of leadership. Once they feel safe in a position or job description, they may stop growing and think of the next step as some far-off eventuality that they don't need to worry about today.

With this mindset, they miss many opportunities, whether it's optimizing their retirement or making their move up the corporate ladder!

The work to get to where you are now has been completed. Your job now is to *get to the next place you want to be.*

Make time for it. Don't let your performance of your current responsibilities slip, but always ensure you have time for *more.*

Decide where you want to be in five years. Really be ambitious and pipe dream about it. Then, take strategic steps to start getting there *today.*

Model Company Values, Culture and Leadership

No company wants a leader at the top who conflicts with company values, company culture, or the rest of the company leadership.

A company needs its top leaders to align with company values, culture and leadership. That means that if you want to get to the top, you must *embody* these things. The good news is, the same exercises and practices that make you into someone who other leaders want to work with will *also* build your character.

The most powerful form of leadership is leadership by example. Most companies and boards realize that if their company leadership is not modeling positive values and culture in their daily work, ripple effects will be felt throughout the company.

No one wants to work or do business with a company that is grouchy, untrustworthy, or lazy. So as a leader shooting for the top, aim to impress by embodying the positive values which are most important to the company in your daily work life.

Level 4 leaders truly are diamonds in the rough. They may not be immediately recognized for their extreme value, but when they are unearthed they become priceless assets that allow a company to grow. Usually, there are only five to ten Level 4 leaders in an organization. That's how rare they are!

That's because it's hard to get leaders firing on all cylinders related to operational performance *and* leadership performance. As you might have gathered, getting to this level of performance takes a lot of work and many years of experience – and the steps required to do so aren't even taught in most business schools!

When an organization succeeds in placing a conglomeration of Level 4 leaders at the top, the results are massive. When they have leaders who put the company and its stakeholders before their own egos or positions, these companies see positive cultural changes and generate immense value for everyone involved.

The Level 4 leader takes care of the company *and* the people. That's because the Level 4 leader knows that the people *are* the company. Without them, nothing gets done!

Be a Head Coach and Not a Field Player

When evaluating your own leadership level, ask yourself: do I accept my role as a coach – someone who's in charge of training players and coordinating optimal outcomes for our team? Or do I still sometimes act like a player myself – someone whose job it is to actively perform tasks that are actually other people's jobs?

Leaders sometimes mistakenly feel that they are helping the player, or the team, if they take over part of a player's workload. In fact, the opposite is true! Players can't thrive and grow if they aren't given independence and responsibility, and a bad coach can actually interfere with the play in progress by getting on the field.

Pittsburgh Steelers head coach Mike Tomlin once forgot his position as a head coach and jumped onto the field, attempting to save a play himself. The result? He tripped an active player, damaging his team's reputation and incurring a fine of $100,000 himself.[26]

On another occasion, Tomlin tried to take over someone else's job territory – in this case, the referee's – and was fined another $25,000 for publicly disagreeing with the judgment of a referee, upon whose objectivity the entire game was based.[27]

In both cases, Tomlin *meant* well. He wanted to help his team succeed. But he forgot his own role and duties and became the guy nobody wants to work with: the one who interferes with his teammates' work and steps on his peers' toes, even spreading word publicly that he doesn't think they're doing their jobs properly!

How likely is a person like that to get promoted to the C-suite? Who would want him in charge of their company, or on their board of directors?

We all have a strong impulse to simply *fix* a problem if we see it. This especially goes for me, the "Resolution Driver."

And yet, we all must be mindful that the way to develop other leaders and move up the corporate ladder ourselves is not to micromanage others or make ourselves "indispensable" in our current positions. Instead, it's to show that we can train great leaders to replace us – and, having mastered this skill of long-term foresight, we deserve to be put in positions of higher responsibility.

Giving up control is hard for everyone. This is why there are so few Level 4 leaders in companies. But to create ongoing growth for *everyone,* we must know when it's time to transition into higher roles. To move forward, we must allow others to do what we have spent most of our career getting good at, or have learned to depend on ourselves to do.

Level 4 leaders know when it's time to "hang up the cleats."

---

[26] Maquinana, R. (2014, February 9). Mike Tomlin fined $100,000 for actions in Steelers' loss. Retrieved from http://www.nfl.com/news/story/0ap2000000292517/article/mike-tomlin-fined-100000-for-actions-in-steelers-loss

[27] Shook, N. (2018, October 10). NFL fines Mike Tomlin $25K for criticism of officials. Retrieved from http://www.nfl.com/news/story/0ap3000000972507/article/nfl-fines-mike-tomlin-25k-for-criticism-of-officials

They leaders know that they are being compensated based on their overall department's contribution and not how many hours their butt, personally, is in their seat! Level 4 leaders depend on their team to perform, holding them accountable but *not* jumping back onto the field.

Balancing the paradoxes of support for their players with holding players accountable for high expectations is one more art of mastery which Level 4 leaders actively practice and perfect.

Peak Level 5 Leader: #1 Company Steward

Organizations must earn money in order to continue to exist. For an organization, having positive cash flow is as essential as breathing. The moment it runs out of money/oxygen to supply to its cells – its workers and supply chains – it begins to die within minutes. Almost immediately, it loses the ability to do the work it must do to stay alive.

I remind us of this here because, as we move up the leadership ladder, we are talking about an increasing number of responsibilities *that are not directly financial.* We have spoken, and will continue to speak, about high-minded ideals of leadership, culture, and teamwork. *But this does not mean we can afford to forget the basic financials that make the world go round.*

All of these skills *can* help us optimize financials. That is their entire point. But just as it is possible to take our eyes off long-term growth because we're staring at our budget for this quarter, it's also sometimes possible to run out of gas – or money – because we are overly focused on a distant goal and not focused enough on this quarter's financials.

With that reminder that *all other skills must be mastered to get to this point*, we will now discuss the rare bird that is the Level 5 Leader.

A Level 5 Leader is someone who has mastered all of the skills discussed at the previous levels of business acumen and leadership, and has now reached a point where they can be trusted with the entire organization's future. In an ideal world, the Level 5 Leader is the

CEO who is answerable to no one except the board and stakeholders who evaluate the company's overall value to the public.

A leader with this level of mastery is unlikely to concern herself with the day-to-day operations of the organization such as salary, personnel decisions, or departmental cashflow unless acute problems arise which are big enough to require her attention.

Instead, she focuses on managing high-level, big-picture matters that determine a company's value to the public such as mission, vision, culture, and customer relations, while trusting lower-level officers to ensure that these ideas are enacted in a financially responsible way and that any problems are brought to her attention.

To become a Level 5 Leader, you must have *first* mastered financial strategy and cashflow skills. However, as a Level 5 Leader, money may not be your primary day-to-day concern. Free from the need to worry about exact dollar amounts on a daily basis, you can now focus on *creating value* – creating experiences and products that people will want to trade money for.

The goal of these ideas, of course, is always *to make money*. All mission, vision, culture, or personnel decisions aim to provide more value to the consumer, and receive more money in exchange. But the question of "how do we do this in the most cost-effective way?" may not be as close at hand for the Level 5 Leader with the 100,000-yard view and the 10-year plan as it might be for her subordinates who work with salaries and budgets directly.

Now, some people have the idea that CEOs are – and should be – dictators. That since no one can say "no" to them except the board and shareholders, the can, and should, rule with an iron fist.

Can you guess what I'm going to say about that? That's right – that's absolutely *not* the case. Being a dictator just because you *can* doesn't yield peak results from your team at the CEO level any more than it does at the middle management level.

Instead, a truly masterful Level 5 Leader understands *all* of the skills we've discussed so far – including how to motivate people, resolve conflicts, and unlock their team's true potential through positive motivation instead of threats and punishments

In my experience, *most* CEOs understand this. In many cases, indeed, this is how they *get* to be CEOs. Level 5 leaders know that they must, at all costs, take care of company profits first. And that is not actually accomplished by running a company based on fear which, as we've seen, actually disengages employees and results in lower productivity.

Remember: Company Profits Are The Lifeblood Of Your Organization

They Allow:

- People to be employed
- People to receive paychecks to take care of their families
- People to be hired
- People and organizations to grow
- Us to measure if we are providing real value to consumers
- Us to determine if we need to change

To some, it might seem that focusing on company profits takes away from the human element of customer relations, or employee-employer relations. But in reality, the opposite is true.

Great leaders who have mastered paradoxes know that *the best profits occur* when customers and employees are truly, ecstatically happy. And that likewise, profit margin is necessary to continue *making* people happy.

This is one more paradox which true leaders must seek to master: "people" and "profits" may seem antithetical to each other to a beginner, but a master sees that each relies on the other for its own prosperity.

A peak-level leader knows that they must maintain the balance of caring both profits and people, and they *cannot successfully do either unless they are doing both.*

The ultimate test of a Level 5 Leader is this: what if they have to fire a friend or family member because that person is damaging the company's culture or its bottom line?

The true sign of a Level 5 Leader is the willingness to make a great personal sacrifice for the good of the company and the people in it.

A Peak Level 5 Leader must *also be* the leader when it comes to Organizational Health!

As we have seen here, there are many ways for organizations to "go wrong" and end up putting forth substandard performance. A Level 5 Leader must be a leader in identifying these obstacles and resolving them where they exist.

If the leaders at lower levels are proactively doing the same thing, so much the better; they are well on their way to becoming Level 5 Leaders. But if the CEO is not doing the same thing, there's only so much the departmental heads can do!

This means that a Level 5 Leader must always:

1. Think about the 'whole body' of the organization instead of only considering its parts in isolation from each other.
2. Develop and maintain a healthy culture that promotes healthy values.
3. Ensure their departments are clear on their own mission and vision and how they fit into the overarching company mission and vision.
4. Ensure their leaders *both* take care of the company *and* their people.
5. Have a high level of personal accountability, and expect the same of their direct reports.
6. Ensure that people are clear on their roles, responsibilities and how they personally contribute to efficiencies, infrastructure or the bottom line.
7. Appropriately recognize individuals, teams and departments for their wins.
8. Are transparent, realistic and honest about past, current and future performance.
9. Are transparent, realistic and honest about necessary changes to the organization.

10. Provide the support and resources necessary for the company to perform.

You can use the SAOL Leadership Ladder as your organization's guideline for developing a strong leadership bench.

As a leader, regardless of our current level of skill, it is always our responsibility to approach our superiors with a desire and a plan to further enhance our skillsets.

Leaders who do this inspire higher performance in themselves and others, and are seen as people who take an active interest in the company's welfare – regardless of their job title.

If we wish to describe ourselves as an effective company leader, this SAOL Leadership Ladder must become our dynamic leadership template for developing *every* leader within our organization.

As leadership mentor John Maxwell observes, *"A leader is one who knows the way, goes the way, and shows the way."*[28]

Dream a bit: What would be the impact in our organization if we did everything in our power to help ourselves and our organization's leaders embody this principle and "move up the ladder?" What would then be possible for us?

---

[28] Maxwell, J. C. (2013). *The 5 Levels of Leadership: Proven Steps to Maximize Your Potential*. New York: Center Street.

Chapter 16

The 8 Essential Qualities of Emotional Intelligence

There is no better way to talk about emotional intelligence and leadership than by sharing a simple LEAD matrix that I've created for my clients.

Simply focus seriously on each of these areas for the rest of your life and work at getting at least a 'C' grade in every area! It's hard work, but you will be amazed by how your life changes when you do this.

- ❑ Do you model leadership today?
- ❑ Do people trust, respect and like to work with you overall?
- ❑ Do you empower yourself?
- ❑ Do you empower others?
- ❑ Are you aware of who you are and what makes you tick?
- ❑ Are you aware of who others and what makes *them* tick?
- ❑ Do you continually develop yourself?
- ❑ Do you help develop others?

Truth: The road to becoming your highest self is a lonely one. It means doing lots of hard work of self-reflection, and never compromising with those who may wish to take the easy way out.

No matter, go for it! The rewards are priceless. The peace of mind and joy that you will eventually bring yourself and others cannot be replaced.

THE 8 ESSENTIAL QUALITIES OF EMOTIONAL INTELLIGENCE		
L	Leader of Self	Leader of Others
	I model leadership	People trust, respect and like to work with me.
E	Empowerer of Self	Empowerer of Others
	I am able to remove barriers that limit my growth.	I am able to help remove barriers that limit other's growth.
A	Awareness of Self	Awareness of Others
	I know who I am and have mastery over my emotions and behavior.	I understand others and can effectively compliment my behavior to work with them.
D	Developer of Self	Developer of Others
	I continually strive to become my 'Highest Self'	I consistently help others become their 'Highest Self'
Created by Rubi Ho, Creator of the SAOL Organizational Leadership Methodology		

Putting It All Together

I'll be 49 years old in a few months. I am blessed to have accomplished many of my goals, but I know I have not yet even touched the tip of the iceberg. As Robert Frost would say: "I have miles to go before I sleep."

For all that I dole out my advice and council, I unabashedly say that I work on all the above incessantly. This, in fact, is what is necessary.

Master athletes become great only by practicing their skill for hours each and every day, and building all of their daily choices around optimizing their performance. Exactly the same holds true for masters in the arena of business.

The principles I write about are not one-time things, but must always be worked and revisited, every single day. In order to thrive and win in life and work, you must make getting better and becoming your highest self as essential and automatic as eating and breathing.

Sound like a tall order? It is. And the results are spectacular.

No one is *ever* "at the finish line." But speaking from experience both personally and professionally, there is *nothing* more gratifying than seeing people's lives get better emotionally, physically and spiritually as a result of daily dedication to their goals.

We'll now move into a discussion that might come as a welcome respite from all this talk of putting your company first: **a discussion of how you can apply the same principles** *to your personal goals,* and some tricks I've found for finding which personal goals bring me the most peace and fulfillment.

I've created an Organizational, Work map for you – on use for your personal life and goals! By using the SAOL mindset and methodology, you tackle the critical areas of work that ultimately lead to your success both personally and professionally, both for your family and your business.

As a recap, the critical areas of your business work map include:

- **Company**: This is where we have focused on Mission, Vision, Strategies, and your Core Competencies.
- **Stakeholder**: Here, we focused on what it takes to develop your peer to peer relationships, and how to best support your peers' needs.
- **Functions and Departments**: This is where we looked at your infrastructure, your processes, and your systems and how we can best optimize them and maximize your efficiencies.
- **Teams**: We've examined what it takes to create a winning, high performing team.
- **Individual**: We took a hard look at the optimal leadership qualities and what it takes to be viewed as a "key player" at work.

As we now dive into your **Life Map**, we will apply the *same* SAOL mindset of mastery to care for six *other* areas – areas dedicated to your own personal well-being and joy.

We will now explore how to thrive, not just in business outcomes, but in your personal life as well.

Chapter 17

BEFORE Creating Your Life Map

Where Are You Now?

The Life Map is a tool I've designed to help you get to where you want to be in life. But to get there from here we must first know where we are right now.

Simply put, where are you *not* thriving?

Your work life might be your major source of anxiety. Or perhaps it's something completely different, like physical health or relationships. Start where your pain is the greatest.

Why? Because pain is the compass that points us toward healing. Until you confront the life areas where your pain is greatest, you will always be limited!

This is the reason I wrote "Confronting My Elephants." For me, my biggest "pain point" was my addiction to money, and my need to be "good enough."

> **For many years, money and pursuing it was my way. It overpowered everything else, and it was a hunger that was never satisfied. Until I overcame my money addiction, I was limited in my ability to experience true peace.**

For many years, money and pursuing it was my way. It overpowered everything else, and it was a hunger that was never satisfied. Until I overcame my money addiction, I was limited in my ability to experience true peace.

Your own pain points may be similar to mine, or they may be different.

In the chapters to come, we are going to explore some tools to help you determine where you are, and what your best route is to peace and happiness – whatever that looks like for you.

Your Checklist

In the chapters to come, we'll introduce you to six areas of life development which, taken together, add up to health, security, fulfillment, and happiness.

We'll move up Maslow's hierarchy of needs, starting with those areas which will cause immediate, acute problems if they are not met and ending with those which provide the most complete fulfillment. All of these are designed to be useful to *all* people, regardless of your current situation or beliefs. These are:

- Physical Health
- Mental Health
- Financial Health
- Relationship Health
- Area of Service
- Spiritual Health

When evaluating these areas, don't think about making your boss, company, partner, parents, pastor, or society in general happy. Don't think about meeting any external metrics or earning accolades.

We're not talking about running a business with stakeholders here: we're talking about running *your life*. The goal of this Life Map is to fill *you* up with health and satisfaction, not to make you "the perfect human being" by anyone else's standards.

Of course, it is quite possible that your own fulfillment also involves making other people in your life happy. It is part of happiness to have people in our lives who care about our well-being and want us to be joyful.

But don't let anybody else's opinions *determine what feels best to you*. Instead, use your own feelings to determine how fulfilled you are, rather than any measurement you've read about or seen on TV.

When creating your own Life Map for each of the six areas, I recommend that you follow the following steps:

- ❑ Assess how fulfilled or not each area feels today
- ❑ Create your goals for the year in each area
- ❑ Create a road-map for each area
- ❑ Reassess once per month and track progress

You may wish to share your goals with the significant people in your life. You might even inspire them to do the same. Me and my entire family have been using Life Maps for over five years. I, personally having been doing them for over a decade.

The results have been unbelievable. I've personally accomplished over 80% of what I set out to achieve in my life, and I'm not done yet!

How is it possible to achieve so much? Well, part of happiness is sorting *what really makes you happy* from the countless, impossible ideals that the culture and people around you may have.

The Truth About Happiness

Take a look at TV ads, the Internet and social media. What do you see? You are urged to buy more, more, more!

You need this, this and this so you can truly feel good about yourself! Happiness means having it all – all the money, all the items, all the experiences – and that is a constantly expanding definition that you can never meet.

At least, that's what the people who are selling those things want you to believe. Fear of n*ot having enough* and *not being good* enough wreak havoc throughout the planet. Even when we reach heights we once thought impossible, it's easy to still feel that we don't "have it all."

It's easy to succumb to always wanting more. I sure succumbed to it.

I grew up poor. Like, really poor. When the vacuum broke in our house, we had to use the broom to sweep dirt from the carpet. All my clothes growing up were hand-me-downs from my older brothers. My socks usually had holes in them because we couldn't afford to continually replace them. I had to walk everywhere or take the bus because our only car was used by my mother to take her to and from her full-time, low-wage job cleaning offices and schools.

With my mother making only minimum wage while supporting eight children, we received food stamps to help supplement my mom's income. Living in a middle class neighborhood where we'd been rented a house at well below-market rates by our church sponsor, we stood out like sore thumbs.

I was always acutely aware of being "the poor kid," and of the vague suspicion our neighbors had about our family living in a house we should not have been able to afford. It wasn't hard to see that I just "didn't belong."

Even with the help of our church community, we barely got by. With her meager wages my mom had to pay for our food, clothes, utilities, school supplies, and transportation as best she could.

There was *no* extra money. For as long as I could remember, our food staples were rice with a little bit of meat and some vegetables. We couldn't afford anything else. I'm not exaggerating.

I share all this because at age five, I was already developing a "keeping up with the Joneses" complex. From my neighbors and classmates, I picked up many ideas about what it meant to be "normal" and "successful," and to have the lifestyle an American was "supposed to have."

Almost all of those ideas revolved around buying and owning things. Society did not help me to suppress this temptation.

I focused on what my family didn't have and what all other families did have. In short order, making money, working, and having things became an obsession of mine. This continued for a good part of my life, driving my desire to learn business skills despite having no money for extracurriculars or paid classes, and the necessity of starting low-wage jobs to support myself as soon as I was legally able.

At eight years old, I started mowing lawns, raking leaves, shoveling snow and baby-sitting. Even at that tender age, I felt I needed to start making my own money to buy things. Comparing my toys, clothes, and bedroom to those of my friends from our middle class school district created a huge inferiority complex in me. They had "the right stuff," literally. I did not have the right stuff, and therefore there was something wrong with *me*.

Despite being seemingly fated for low-paying jobs that did not require formal education, I swore to myself that I wasn't going to be part of the "have nots" if I had anything to do with it.

For a short time, this obsession served me well. It allowed me to put almost superhuman effort into learning business and negotiation skills.

Unfortunately, I later learned that there was *no* satisfying this craving to "keep up with the Joneses," no matter how successful I was. There was no happiness when I was trying to "have it all."

I started applying for credit cards as soon as I was old enough to qualify. I took out loans, worked multiple jobs, and still spent more than I was making. I promised myself I would "catch up" after I had "the right stuff." I was living way beyond my means, not out of lust for pleasure, but out of *anxiety*.

I couldn't let myself *look* unsuccessful to others by lacking material possessions. The more successful I *looked*, I reasoned, the more money people would be willing to pay me.

Before long, I was writing credit card checks to pay for credit card bills. I submerged myself into massive debt.

At the pinnacle of my debt accumulation, I was $3.3 million in debt. I had student loans, car loans and credit card debt. I owned 25 units of real estate – which I had bought after calculating that becoming a real estate mogul would be the fastest, easiest way to make enormous amounts of money.

That I never quite managed to make the promised return on investment did not register

> How did I get so lost in my pursuit of success? Easy. I obsessed over what I hadn't had as a child: money and things.

in my mind. My wife and I were paying over \$18,000 a month on bills alone, the bulk of which were mortgage loans from our many properties.

I thought that by acquiring and leveraging properties, I would become a multi-millionaire. That way, I could afford whatever I wanted so I could keep up or ahead of everyone else. That would be the true definition of success, according to the culture I grew up in. I talk about this episode in my life in depth in my autobiographical book, *"Confronting My Elephants."*

Now, this might sound somewhat reasonable to you so far. After all, haven't we talked about money being what makes the world go round? Doesn't everyone know that it's important to negotiate for and optimize your salary and your investments?

More money is good, right? And even making risky investments can lead to a great payoff, right?

Money is a tool. It is not happiness itself. And if you don't use it wisely to create *value* – that is, to create whatever makes you happy – it won't deliver on any of its promises.

After all, when we create value for customers in business, we are not *giving them money*. We are giving them an *experience* that makes them *happy*. Savvy consumers trade money for happiness, and they do this by knowing what *actually* makes them happy and recognizing money as a means to that end.

As a money addict, I had the "money" part down, but not the happiness. As a result, my life was a mess.

At the time I believed that if I could have what the Joneses had, I would be happy. If I could have the nice car, the nice house, the nice clothes, the nice things, then I would be well-respected, and I would be happy.

But the opposite happened. I was miserable. I was stressed. I was anxious. Sure, it made me feel good when people complimented me on my things, but those feelings were only temporary. They never lasted. The anxiety far outweighed the joy.

At thirty-three, after having immersed myself in the dream of keeping up with the Joneses for my entire life in America, I had finally had enough.

Deciding this was a pivotal moment for me. Money didn't automatically create happiness, so what did? Money didn't define me or make me a happy person – so what did? Who was I, really? What was *my* definition of happiness and success?

That's when I started looking *much* more deeply within myself, seeking to define who I authentically was. I spent *much* less time looking outward to advertisements and examples of wealthy people for what I "should" become.

I'm no minimalist. If things make you happy, go for it. But keep your eye on the happiness meter – not the money and expense meter.

Just because something is expensive or prestigious doesn't *necessarily* mean that it will make you happy. And just because something is minimalist or isn't expensive, doesn't mean it is bad!

There is no external thing that can define *who we really are*. There is no little vial labeled "happiness" that we can buy. Instead, our identity and happiness come *from within*. Money doesn't always have to interfere with that – but it certainly doesn't automatically give these things to us, either.

How did I get so lost in my pursuit of success? Easy. I obsessed over what I hadn't had as a child: money and things. The deficits in what I owned as a child were so big that they formed my entire self-concept and definition of success. But one day, I hit a point where this simply stopped working.

Those "low points" that make us realize our current approach is never going to work are a tremendous gift.

Regaining and Maintaining Perspective: What Really Matters?

I found out that money and material wealth did not define me or make me happy. The same, I can say with complete confidence, is true for you.

So what *does* define a person? What does bring true happiness?

The psychologist Abraham Maslow did pioneering work in

studying what made people really happy. He found, unsurprisingly, that people were generally happier when they had their basic physical survival needs such as food and water met, and when they were safe – that is, they didn't need to worry about being attacked or harmed at any moment.

Most of us in the U.S. have that, yet many of us are not breathtakingly thrilled with our daily lives. So what else is needed?

Maslow found that, after not being in physical danger, the most important determiners of human happiness were love and belonging, respect and self-esteem, and something called self-actualization. As the name suggests, self-actualization consisted of becoming one's highest self.[29] Notice that none of those are things you can buy on Amazon.

> I am sharing all of this science with you because it backs up what sages and mystics have been saying for millennia: that we are most fulfilled when we are fulfilling our true purpose, and that our true purpose is helping others.

Subsequent work by other psychologists has shown that almost all of our happiness comes from having meaningful relationships and doing meaningful work. Indeed, studies have found that stress levels and even mortality levels are lower in people who have warm, intimate, positive family and social relationships.[30] In job satisfaction studies, life satisfaction is higher and mortality rates are lower when people feel that their work is "meaningful," which is usually defined as "having a positive impact on other people's lives."[31]

In fact, some psychologists have gone so far as to frame the needs for love, belonging, and meaningful purpose as being a new category of survival needs. After all, our ancestors depended on

[29] Mcleod, S. (2018, May 21)..Maslow's Hierarchy of Needs. Retrieved from https://www.simplypsychology.org/maslow.html
[30] Holt-Lunstad, J., Smith, T., & Layton, J. (2010). Social Relationships and Mortality Risk: A Meta-analytic Review. *SciVee*. doi: 10.4016/19865.01
[31] More Than Job Satisfaction. (n.d.). Retrieved from https://www.apa.org/monitor/2013/12/job-satisfaction

mutual assistance and teamwork to obtain food, safety, and the most basic survival needs. We survived as a species despite our relative lack of teeth and claws because we loved helping others, and we often relied on mutual assistance to survive.

It would make sense, then, for our brains and bodies to view rejection, loneliness, and behavior that is harmful toward others as being *just as stressful* as lack of food or physical danger.[32]

Recent advances in measuring stress hormones and brain activity have found that social rejection can register as just as painful as fear of dying, and that people actually physically grow and heal more effectively when they have a sense of purpose serving others.

I am sharing all of this science with you because it backs up what sages and mystics have been saying for millennia: that we are most fulfilled when we are fulfilling our true purpose, and that our true purpose is helping others.

This is how we acquire Maslow's senses of love and belonging, respect and self-esteem, and self-actualization. This is how we form warm, intimate relationships, come to be respected as upstanding and highly capable individuals, and develop our skills and purpose to a high level.

And this all lines up with some other interesting recent findings. Psychologists have found that using money to buy activities or classes *makes people happier* than using money to buy items.[33]

It's as though putting our money toward experiences that can give us love, belonging, respect, self-esteem, and self-actualization *really does* make people happier than buying clothes, fast cars, or houses, which appear nowhere on Maslow's pyramid.

Again, I have no problem with owning these things. I own some of them myself. But I now know why I was so unhappy before.

---

[32] The Thing We Fear More Than Death. (n.d.). Retrieved from https://www.psychologytoday.com/us/blog/the-real-story-risk/201211/the-thing-we-fear-more-death

[33] Pozin, I. (2016, March 4). The Secret to Happiness? Spend Money on Experiences, Not Things. Retrieved from https://www.forbes.com/sites/ilyapozin/2016/03/03/the-secret-to-happiness-spend-money-on-experiences-not-things/

I learned – and science agrees with me – that owning *stuff* and having huge numbers in my bank account are not my best return on investment for happiness.

Instead, my best return on investment for happiness is *my ability to serve others*.

This is a Biblical idea, and a Buddhist one, and any other religion you might care to name. But it is also now supported by science, in fields as diverse as workplace satisfaction, studies of stress hormones and brain activity, and overall well-being and mortality studies.

We don't need to rely on scientific statistics to tell us how to be happy. That answer is right within ourselves. But it helps to have the external validation, in a world where constant messages that we need "more, more, more" are coming at us from every direction.

In fact, society wants to convince you that you will *never* have enough. And as long as you succumb to the temptation to believe them when they say you'll feel better if you buy more things, you'll *never* reach self-actualization! You'll be spending your resources in all the wrong places.

Oh, you have clothes? Well now you need nicer ones. Oh, you've attained food? Now you need different and *better* types of food. Oh, you have a car? Well now you need to have a better car.

Oh, you have a house? Oh, you've found a job? Well now you need a better-paying job. Now you need a *bigger* house, or another vacation home in a more glamorous location.

My question for you is this: When does the cycle stop? When do you have *enough*?

If it were up to society, you would *never* have enough and you should *never* stop attaining and acquiring. If this really made you happy, it would be fine. But many of us already know from experience that this is not where true happiness comes from.

One global study a few years back in 2015 determined that money *can* make people happier by helping them to meet their basic needs and acquire tools for self-actualization. But after a certain threshold ($75,000/year in 2015), making more money did not increase a person's happiness at all. *Forbes* recently updated that number to

$95,000 to reflect changes in inflation and costs of living since 2015.[34]

This shows that while money *can* be used as a tool, millions or billions of dollars are not actually necessary for happiness. In fact, as long as a person's basic physical needs are met, having more money doesn't seem to meaningfully affect happiness at all.

To be clear, have at it if you are one of those who has the aspirational goal of becoming a multi-millionaire or billionaire. There are certainly ways to use that money to serve others and help them meet their own hierarchy of needs– thereby obtaining love, belonging, etc..

But money is not the *only* way to obtain those things, and it likely won't buy happiness if it isn't used to do so.

The bottom line is that money is a means to an end, but *real* happiness has more to do with one's relationships, self-worth, and ability to serve others. In other words:

SELF WORTH IS REAL WORTH!

Growing up in the 70's, just having come out of the Vietnam War, there were Americans who embraced my family and Americans who didn't. Some had the natural human desire to help us, while others saw us as members of "the enemy camp" or were afraid of us because we were unfamiliar to them.

And adult's views spilled over to their kids. In school, I would get bombarded every now and then with taunts of: "Chink, go to back to your country!" or hostile or fearful looks in the school cafeteria.

On the outside, I didn't flinch. Inside however, I felt like I was dying. To be told that I didn't belong, or that I was scary and dangerous, *hurt*. We all learn about the world from hearing what other people say, and there was a part of me that actually *believed* I was inferior.

I'd be lying to you if I told that I've completely overcome my

---

[34] This Is The New Price Of Happiness - Forbes. (n.d.). Retrieved from https://www.forbes.com/sites/learnvest/2018/02/19/this-is-the-new-price-of-happiness/

inferiority complex. I haven't. But I do know I'm much further along because I've conscientiously worked on it my whole life.

I am now more able to understand my true worth – and better able to serve others because of it.

It's amazing how much we allow others to tell us who we are! Our brains are made to learn from people who might have knowledge we don't. They are also made to pay more attention to negative information that is scary than to positive, good news – because in the jungle, "bad news" could mean a tiger is chasing us, which needs to be attended to immediately. But sometimes, our brains take this a little too far!

For example, I could have a hundred clients say that they *love* my work and my service that I provide to them. I could be riding on a high, for at least a moment or two. Yet it only takes one criticism or negative comment from one client and I quickly get down in the dumps.

I wish this weren't true, but it is. I eventually recover, but I know I still have miles to go before I can simply just brush off the negative nellies!

This is something many of us experience, and it can make it harder for us to maintain our self-worth. It can even make it easier for us to buy into the idea that if we *buy more stuff*, or *look* more like successful people, we will feel better or have more worth.

I use the following tricks to keep my 'you are not good enough' demons at bay:

1. **Ask your kids and your spouse what they value MOST about you.** Really listen and take notes. I'll bet they won't say your car, your job or nice clothes!

2. **Read scripture or your favorite spiritual book on what is prized most in life.** You'll find there are remarkable similarities between the statements of wise people across cultures, continents, and centuries. And you'll find that they agree especially on one thing: what is most valuable in life has *nothing* with how much you make or the title or position that

you have, no matter how important you might feel because of them.

3. **Get a life coach.** A good one is priceless. He can guide us to embrace our true worth. Sometimes we are so lost within ourselves that we need to be jolted out by an external source. A great life coach can do this for you!

4. **Give.** There is no greater way to start detaching from things than to start giving things away. You can start small. Eventually, speaking from personal experience, you won't be phased about what you *don't have or do have.* A thing is simply a means to an end. Nothing more. Nothing less.

5. **Get away from the Joneses.** We become like the five people we hang around with the most. Sometimes the only way you can change directions is by changing who we spend our time with. If the people in your life are dragging you into the not-good-enough abyss, you need to cut ties! If not, you will drown just like them. **This is critical. Harmful behaviors spread like the most contagious viruses.**

6. **Take a "need versus want" inventory of *everything* you have!** You may discover that you actually *need* very little. Ask yourself simple questions. What do these things do for your self-worth? Do you really need that car or do you just really want that car? Do you really need the fifth TV or do you really want it? Some people even find that they are more satisfied when they narrow their possessions down to only those things which bring them the *most* joy, and use those more often!

7. **Wait to buy that thing you believe you really can't live without. Take a few days or even weeks to make a decision.** Some financial debt-free programs have you freeze your credit card. This is to help you avoid the impulse buy! Remember, society and media are *very* skilled at making you feel that everyone has this thing, why shouldn't you? Yet very often if you put off your decision to buy for a few days or weeks, you

will look back and wonder why you ever wanted that thing in the first place.

8. **Have a garage sale.** You'll quickly realize how many of the things you thought you valued weren't that valuable after all. This is especially true when you start going through your possessions – and start finding things you didn't even remember that you had! There will be things you've held on to that no one will buy, even at a garage sale. This helps us learn to ask "will I even want this in a few months, or will it just become more junk that is a burden to me?"

9. **Get 100 percent debt-free; owe nothing, including your house and see how happy you get!** My wife and I had a mantra at the time I was 33 years old and enveloped in debt: "debt-free by 43." Relentlessly and with vigilance, we tackled our debts, all of them and did everything we could to free ourselves from any sort of financial burden. A big part of this was cutting our spending on needless things using the tricks above. Instead of buying new things, we focused on paying off the things we had *already* bought – and found that we were actually happier for it!

   Today, we have no debts. Even our house is completely paid off. Being debt free drastically reduces any sense of obligation to others, and definitely helps keep my "not good enough" demons at bay.

10. **Make a list of the MOST important things in your life and share it with those you love!** In May, 1996, Eric Clapton's house was burning down. As soon as he caught wind of this, he ran into the blazing fire for his guitars! Out of all the things he had, which I'm sure numbered in the millions, he was just worried about his guitars! That's it! Everything else he owned was ultimately unimportant to his happiness.

Like Eric, I'm sure some things will make our "most important" list But I'm willing to bet that *most* of the things you own do not meaningfully increase your happiness.

Take an inventory. Reflect on it. Challenge it. And start to value the real you, which is *way* beyond the things you have!

I'll sound like a broken record here, but so be it. This is important. So many people struggle financially – all while buying things that don't meaningfully contribute to their happiness!

When we succumb to what society says we need and are, our chances of finding ourselves and realizing what we are really worth is 0 percent. Sooner rather than later, shed anything that is your false self and embrace your true self.

> Said differently, *always* strive to become your perfect, highest self in every way, realizing it's going to be an imperfect, ongoing journey your whole life. Enjoy the ride!

What's the litmus test? As you are taking an inventory of your things, simply ask:

- Why am I really doing what I'm doing?
- Why do I have this title?
- Why do I have these things?
- Are they truly for my own satisfaction?
- Am I trying to project to others that I am just as good as them?
- Are they a need, or simply a want?

Work on Loving Your Imperfect Self Every Day!

Here again, it might sound like I'm talking out of both sides of my mouth. This book is primarily about what you *should* do to improve your personal outcomes.

How then, can I tell you to love your imperfections and accept yourself as you are every day?

I've said before that the discipline of masters lies in perfecting the balance between paradoxical ideas. Often if we cannot embrace both sides of the paradox, we cannot have success!

Said differently, *always* strive to become your perfect, highest self in every way, realizing it's going to be an imperfect, ongoing journey your whole life. Enjoy the bumpy ride!

If we cannot love ourselves as we are and accept our seeming "imperfections," we cannot discover our true Superpower. We also cannot cultivate many of the other skills in this book unless we are coming from a place of genuine self-acceptance and sincere self-love.

Why? It is necessary for us to treat ourselves as the most important person in the world *because we are the only person we are in charge of.*

We are the only person whose health and wellness determines our ability to perform and serve others. We are the only person whose happiness and contentment we can directly steward. We are the only person whose skills we get to use and develop. When we neglect our self-love and self-care, we end up placing that burden upon other people.

So get as many self-help, self-loving books, audibles, and sources you need to be able to continually work on the most important person in the world - you! You'll know you are making progress because you'll be able to laugh at yourself with genuine mirth! Don't ever stop. You *are* worth it!

Regardless of which methods you choose to love and care for yourself, they key is to work on self-worth daily.

You can't miss even one day without consequences. We are *that* vulnerable and susceptible to self-doubt, insecurities, workaholism – and other evils that will render us less able to achieve our goals or care for others. If you take the time to establish firm self-worth until your cup is full, you will reap the benefits for the rest of your life.

On the subject of filling your cup, it helps if you...

Find Time To Do What You Love - Even If You're Not Getting Paid

"Do what you love."

· Once, we were widely advised to make careers out of our hobbies and passions. Sometimes, that's a great thing to do. For those of us who are driven in that direction, it can allow us to provide unique and amazing services using our Superpower, and devote our whole lives to our crafts.

But it can also lead to a slippery slope: once we start thinking of our passions and careers as the same, we start applying financial calculations to them. It can be easy to forget why we loved to do these things in the first place – and then the things we love have lost their true value.

So find time to do the things you love – *without* worrying about whether it's immediately financially profitable.

It *is* so critical that you *do* what you love, regardless of whether or not you can make a living at it. As we've mentioned earlier, money isn't the *only* form of value. It is a means to an end: not "points in the game of life."

So make sure you are filling your life with *value* – whatever fills you with joy. Life's just too short to move through it without doing things that are meaningful or enjoyable to you.

Take it from me. I had to flee my home country, leaving two sisters behind because we could not obtain transport for them. I then had to start over from scratch, struggle to stay afloat, just to have his mom die suddenly and have no father around to help in any way, shape, or form.

Life is short. It is fragile. Its value is measured not by numbers in a bank account, but by the *value* you create.

What is valuable to you?

Doing what you love is an absolute need and *not* a mere want of the human spirit. The human spirit is designed to many things, and these *needs* have created culture across the millennia. Your heart needs to sing.

Wayne Dyer, a spiritual author and speaker, often preached: "Don't let your internal flame die within you."[35] I wholeheartedly agree. Our internal flame creates tremendous value for us, and those around us.

---

[35] Dyer, W. W. (2016). *10 Secrets for Success and Inner Peace*. Carlsbad, CA: Hay House, Inc.

One of my older brothers is world-renowned artist Quang Ho. Since he was a little kid, he always knew he was going to be an artist. He knew what lit his fire *never* veered from this path.

Until he made it in a field that often pays starvation wages, however, he had to hold down a number of jobs to pay the bills. I remember him being everything from a pizza delivery person to a school janitor to an apprentice for a graphics design company to a comic book trader.

Some might see these as "poor" choices because they were not the most financially lucrative jobs available to him. But he knew that his work was creating *value* – a different kind of value from the monetary kind. And because he knew this, he was able to elevate his craft to the level of mastery which can't be reached with mere financial calculations.

The fact is, he did not allow financial constraints to *stop* him from doing what he loved. In present day now, he has the blessing to make a spectacular living being an artist, creating unique value for millions of people through his work, and has collectors and students from all over the world.

Of course, you don't have to become a professional artist to create value by doing what you love. But my brother's story illustrates that *both* types of value – the financial, and the countless other ways to create and experience profound joy – are important to our own spirit, and even to society.

Obsessed with financial security and money as a status symbol, I chose the more financially lucrative path. But this didn't always light my fire. At first. you could say I was a "walking zombie" around work. I simply followed the money and did whatever I had to do to make a living.

I did landscaping, worked at a music hall, was a telemarketer, delivered papers, sold knives, sold coupon books, worked at a pizza parlor, scooped ice cream, was as a parking lot attendant, taught martial arts, elementary school and high school, purchased real estate, and finally worked at the Fortune 100 employer where I was able to discover that my problem-solving gift could be used to drastically increase profits for even the largest organizations on the planet.

The pivotal "wake up" moment for me was when I realized that, despite having great financial security at my Fortune 100 employer, I wasn't engaged with my daily job duties. More than that, I felt – and was starting to be able to *prove* – that these duties held me back from creating all the value I was able to create.

This showed in the number of "extracurriculars" - endeavors that went above and beyond my actual job description – I had taken on in an attempt to scratch my problem-solving itch. I had already:

- Joined the corporate training division
- Become part of the Asian Pacific American Steering Committee
- Gotten my second master's degree in Organizational Management
- Bought over twenty-five units of real estate
- Created a "Find your Seat on the Bus" leadership program
- Created a "Find your Purpose" program at my church
- Got my executive coaching certification at Penn State

I didn't do those things because I wanted my boss to like me. I was simply unfulfilled and *not* pursuing what I loved, which was optimization, in my daily job duties!

Is that you? Do you find that you give your best in an area outside of work?

If so, make sure that you *value that area*. That may or may not mean finding a job which allows you to truly leverage that spark within. It may simply mean finding a way to elevate your passion to the level of mastery, and use it to inspire others.

Either way, *make sure you cultivate that spark*. Don't let any form of value be lost just because it does not register in your bank account!

My Fortune 100 employer was a great place to work. It had a great company culture and was challenging for me but – but my daily job duties were *not* fulfilling my passion.

What *was* fulfilling me? Any way I could find to help people be better, both at work and in life. That's what started my pursuit of the fields of executive coaching and organizational leadership, and eventually led to me creating my own firm to allow me to create maximum value by doing this full-time.

So ask yourself a few personal questions:

1. What do I love? What do I *really* love? Don't give your "why you should hire me" answer here. Give the true, honest, nobody-listening-but-you-and-God answer.
2. Would it be a good idea for me to make this a career? What would I gain if I did? What would I lose? Would I be able to create more value if I could offer this service to people and companies full-time, or would I best be able to serve myself and others by keeping a different "day job" and keeping my passion free of financial concern?

   Either way – make time to do what you love, regardless of whether or not you can get paid for it. Keep your internal flame alive by finding ways *outside* of work to tap into it directly. Even if you start to do it for a living, make time to perform your passion *without getting paid for it* to ensure that the creative spark remains free. You'll find you'll be much happier for it!
3. Is there somewhere you can volunteer?
4. Are there kids you can mentor?
5. Are there events you can host?
6. Is there somewhere where you can be a coach?
7. Are there people in your community who can benefit from your expertise?
8. Is there a teacher who can nurture your love for music, painting or some other form of art?

Regardless of what your passion and love is, keep it alive and thriving by giving it room to spread its wings.

Alongside my profession, I keep my spark alive and free by doing free consulting work for organizations and people who can't afford my services. I speak four times per year at my church to share my knowledge, write blogs and books, play golf, read spiritual and self-help books, mentor Millennials, and cook. All of these things keep my spirit alive and fill my cup. What fills yours?

Life Lesson: *Just* following the money NEVER pays off. Doing what you love ALWAYS pays off.

The things we love often point us toward our Superpowers. That means they can point us toward the career areas where we will perform best – as well as to certain sources of joy, within or separate from our work lives.

Learn to Embrace Death While You Are Still Alive

Some wise people have asked the question: "What would you do if you knew this was your last day on Earth?"

The reminder that life is short and fragile can be surprisingly beneficial. While our immediate response is anxiety, many of us can then move through this and get to the answer of *what is most important for me to do* or *what makes me the happiest?*

What would you do if it was your last day on Earth? What would you regret not completing? What affairs do you need to get in order? I was forced to reckon with the fragility of life at an early age – even after leaving Vietnam.

It was an early Saturday morning, back in the summer of 1983, when a police officer knocked on the door of our new family home in America. My eldest sister in the States, Sa, answered it. Because my room was right next to our porch, I could see the officer from the corner of my window, and my stomach filled with a feeling of dread. But I could only hear murmurs.

> Life boils down to the experiences you have created with the people you have surrounded yourself with, the service you have provided to others, the time you have spent loving yourself, and the relationship you have developed with the meaning of life.

My older brother, Bao, walked into my room in tears. He said that the officer had informed my sister that my mom had been killed by a drunk driver.

The words hit me like a punch in the stomach. This was not possible! It could not be true!

I looked out of my window and saw my mother's brown Toyota Corolla. Wanting to grasp on any shred of hope I could, I screamed at my brother: "You're a liar! Her car is right outside!"

My brother's lip trembled. "She was in her boyfriend's car, Rubi. They were both hit."

This understanding that life is fragile has guided the way I live my life ever since. And it has changed my life for the better.

We might do our best to delay death by taking care of ourselves and living the best life we can. But ultimately we are *not* able to change the fact that are bodies are going to die one day. To paraphrase the song written by Fred Rose and the late American country music singer-songwriter Hank Williams: "We'll never get out of this life alive!"

We can't add a second to our lives by worrying. But we *can* live several lifetimes at once by living each day to its fullest, whatever that might mean for us.

Life boils down to the experiences you have created with the people you have surrounded yourself with, the service you have provided to others, the time you have spent loving yourself, and the relationship you have developed with the meaning of life.

That's deep, but it's true. In fact, scientists have shown that we can *literally* make our lives seem longer by creating many varied experiences for ourselves. It turns out that our brain measures time by the number of unique events we experience. This is why a single week may feel like a lifetime if we are doing many things we have never done before, yet several months might feel like a few days if we are simply "going through the motions" of a routine.[36]

---

[36] Why Time Goes Faster as You Get Older. (n.d.). Retrieved from https://www.psychologytoday.com/us/ blog/cutting- edge-leadership/201004/ why-time-goes-faster-you-get-older

When we combine this finding with the findings that we feel most fulfilled when serving others, incredible things can happen.

So *how* do you embrace death while you are still alive? First of all, I live my life by something Ghandi once said: "Live as if you were to die tomorrow. Learn as if you were to live forever."

This profound wisdom prepares you for anything. As a matter of fact, that quote is under my picture in my 1989 high school yearbook.

Secondly, my **"Life Map"** is created specifically to address what I have found to be the most important areas for myself, which allow me to have the best experiences and fulfillment. These have the pleasant side effect of also creating great experiences for my loved ones and great service to my community, since the principles of happiness make these all the same endeavor.

Having used this **"Life Map"** for over a decade now, I have had the opportunity to refine the process into a highly functional method. I simply write down goals I'd like to achieve in each area and spend the entire year trying to achieve those goals.

Goals can be monthly, quarterly, or annual – depending on how long it can reasonably be expected to take to achieve them. Just like when planning a strategy in business, we try not to rush the process too much – lest we get inferior results due to haste. But we also hold ourselves accountable when deadlines come around if our goals have not been met.

"Be a better husband to my wife," for example could be an area I write down in my Relationships section. "Meditate daily," could be something I write down in my Spiritual health section, and so forth and so forth.

By requiring me to complete all six areas, I ensure that my growth and well-being is well-balanced – and I'm not being held back in my relationship goals by failure to address a physical health problem, for example. This can be likened to ensuring that every department of your company has what it needs to function optimally, so that no department holds your company's total capabilities back.

The point of the **Life Map** is to put intention and goals behind the critical areas of one's life. Since no one is employed as my "Director of Physical Health," I use the Life Map to continually evaluate myself and determine what needs to be done in each department to make my life better.

I simply ask myself: "What really matters at the end of the day? How can I tap into what really matters on a daily basis?"

These Life Map areas, if focused upon daily, truly do lead to a *rich and fulfilled life.*

Since becoming an orphan, I have been on the search for a mentor who was never there. An adult or someone who could guide me. The reality was, at least for me, there *was* no one. So I put it on myself to become my *own* guide. I found my greatest peace in being intentional about what I've concluded are the *most* important areas in an individual's life.

Since the creation of my Life Map, I can personally attest that I have *never* felt more complete and fulfilled in my life as a whole and sense of direction and purpose. I desire the same for you. **Take time in the following areas, and see if you can complete the personal Life Map for yourself.**

Life Map as a Game Changer: Focus Daily on What's Most Important

Seneca, a Roman philosopher, once wrote, "*If a man does not know to what port he is steering, no wind is favorable to him.*" In other words, if you don't know your destination, you can't make any progress to reach it.

That is the story of my early life. I was lost for a major portion of my childhood and young adult life.

It's amazing what happened to me when I didn't have a strong sense of direction. I was prone to follow any new idea that came along, or anyone who *appeared* to have a firm sense of direction. Because of that, my direction was always changing.

Before I knew it, I looked around and asked: "Where the hell am I? Who the hell am I?" I didn't know.

It is essential that we know to which port we are steering. We must know what destinations will fulfill us or allow us to reach our goals. This requires a map. A Life Map is a compass I created for myself and others, including my coaching clients. It creates a sense of stability and direction for some of the *most* important areas in life. It allows us to choose our destinations with forethought, and reach them faster.

What do we do every day? Who we spend time with? Who do we want to become? What can we leave behind for others?

What do you want to get out of your life? What do you long for in your life? What makes you happy?

Honestly answer these questions and you will be closer to determining what truly counts as important to you.

And remember – we are all made unique *for a reason*. When I say "what is most important *to you*" I am not suggesting that there is nothing that is objectively important. But each of us are gifted with different talents and personalities which allow us to create and experience value *in unique ways*.

Just like knowing your Superpower unlocks your best performance at work because that is what you can do better than anyone else, knowing what brings you joy unlocks the doorway to your richest and most fulfilled life.

What Fulfills You?

I remember one evening after my mother died, sitting out on the porch by myself. I felt tears welling up in my eyes and screamed into the night sky: "How can there be such a thing as a loving God, when you allow a family to be motherless and fatherless, left to struggle and barely stay alive!" It was a dark time for me.

I eventually came to realize that the only thing that really mattered was living a life of fulfillment and purpose. No grieving or crying or anger, no matter how extensive, was going to bring my mom back. I could either continue to sulk or move forward and really live. I chose to really live.

The Life Map operates off two questions: If today was *literally* your last day on Earth,

1. **What would you regret *not* having done today?**
2. **Who would you have regretted *not* having spent time with today?**

No one knows when their last day is going to be. So stop acting like you have limitless time on planet Earth. You don't!

Don't rush the answers to these questions. You want the *best* answers, not the *easiest* ones. Take your time. If it feels right to you, try completing one section of your Life Map each day for a week.

Take a breather. Find a quiet place. Clear your mind. Find a time when you feel your mind is least distracted and most fresh. Find a place where you are comfortable and away from noise and disturbances to work.

Take this work seriously. It's your life. It's your happiness. It's your peace. And yes, you are worth it!

Chapter 18

Creating Your Life Map

Core Area 1: Daily Physical Health Focus

It is hard to do anything if your body and brain are not working well. Remember, both are part of the same system: you're unlikely to be able to function well at work, or have a healthy mood and outlook on life, if your brain and the rest of your body are suffering from untreated illness.

In our culture, too many of us let our physical health go because we tell ourselves it "is not important" or "is not worth taking the time and energy to fix." In reality, studies show that poor physical health impairs our mood and decision-making abilities, not to mention our happiness and well-being![37]

Many of the problems you may think of as mental health problems, or "exhaustion from doing too much" may in fact be solved if you address your physical health. So let's take some time talking about how to do that.

Up until my early thirties I really didn't care about my physical health and nutrition. I used to eat candy constantly, drink soda with every meal, and have late night snacks on a daily basis.

Things changed however, once my son came into my life. I started wondering: "Will I be around to see him grow up? Will I be there to take care of him if he needs me?"

At that point, not having any birth record or medical records due

---

[37] How Health Affects a Child's School Performance. (n.d.). Retrieved from https://health.ucsd.edu/news/2006/Pages/04_07_Taras.aspx

to our fleeing Vietnam, I had no idea. All I knew was that my mother had died young in an accident and my father had not been around.

That's when things started to change for me on the physical and nutrition side. If I didn't want to leave my son the way my parents disappeared from my life, I'd better start taking action to live long!

Fortunately for me, my "resolution driver" skills came in handy here. I used the same sort of data collection for my physical health that I would use to help a company improve its performance.

I started tracking what I ate, and how I felt afterwards. I started watching my energy levels and collecting data on what helped or harmed them. I began learning about nutrition and exercise, and how helpful those things could be to my overall longevity and well-being.

I was lucky to have grown up in a family that valued some of the most effective forms of physical exercise. I'd practiced martial arts for over fourteen years, and as a result had good muscle strength throughout my body, and a quick metabolism.

That didn't mean however, that I had high, sustained, energy levels. At the start of my physical health work, I couldn't understand why I didn't have any stamina. The answer turned out to lie in other areas of physical health such as nutrition and sleep. Who knew?

In Alan Deutschman's book, *Change or Die*, he proved that the only thing that changes and motivates someone to get up and do something is having a sense of purpose and internal motivation.

He studied drug addicts, felons, and cancer patients whose conditions were sometimes induced by voluntary behaviors, and proved time and time again, the sustainable changes in behaviors came from a sense of purpose and motivation rather than education or fear of death.[38]

For me, *that* motivation was my son. What is your physical health motivation?

It could be being around for a child. It could be simply feeling better, more capable, and more optimistic. It could be performing

---

[38] Deutschman, A. (2008). *Change or Die: the Three Keys to Change at Work and in Life*. New York: Collins.

better at work as a result of having better concentration and decision-making.

Your body is the vehicle that takes you everywhere. By maintaining it and maybe even upgrading it, you can reach any goal you might have more quickly.

So ask, what really motivates you?

I promise you, whatever your biggest motivation or goal is – it can be achieved faster through better physical health.

Your Challenge:

Make a list of your physical health concerns or uncertainties, and what you plan to do about them. Include *any* frustrations you might have with the performance of your body or mind, such as exhaustion or stress. I have known quite a few people whose "unavoidable" exhaustion actually stemmed from vitamin deficiencies or treatable hormone conditions!

Then create a timeline with specific goals and share them with others to increase your accountability.

Physical Health Checklist:

- ❑ Where do you want/need to improve physically?
- ❑ What do you want to accomplish in this area in the next year?
- ❑ Do you have a primary care doctor? Have you talked to them about your concerns, symptoms, or what you wish your brain or body could do better?
- ❑ How can I work toward my physical health goals every single day?

Physical health is about taking care of your body, it's the only one you've got in this lifetime. It's the only vehicle you get to take you where you want to go.

What do you need to do this year to make sure your body is as healthy as possible? What can you do to help it take you where you want to go with a sense of ease and wellbeing?

What action can you take to move you toward that goal *each and every day?*

Core Area 2: Your Daily Mental Health Priority

In his book, "The Disappearance of the Universe," Gary R. Renard says: "We will achieve world peace the day the world's people achieve inner peace."[39]

This is very true! It's also true that our mental health can make it difficult for us to function by impairing our mood, outlook on life, and our ability to feel the way we want to feel and do the things we want to do.

In some places, "mental health" is still thought of as a "wishy washy" area of science. But in fact, in recent years scientists have uncovered that our brains and bodies have *measurable physical and chemical responses* to stress. We can even create or alleviate measurable, physical stress on our brains and bodies based on the ways we think, the ways we view ourselves, and the kind of support systems we surround ourselves with.

This is huge news! It means that mental health care and maintenance can have just as big an effect on our performance and well-being as our physical health!

According to the World Health Organization, at least 264 million globally people have depression. Depression is one of the world's leading causes of disability, with millions of people globally feeling too sad, pessimistic, or lonely to do the things they want to do.[40]

We now know that depression is a condition of brain chemistry and gene expression. It's not as simple as "thinking happy thoughts"

---

[39] Renard, G. R. (2010). *The Disappearance of the Universe*. Syndey N.S.W.: RHYW.

[40] Depression. (n.d.). Retrieved from https://www.who.int/news-room/fact-sheets/detail/depression

or "cheering up." But we *also* know that it can be caused or prevented by our environments and experiences.

People who do not have warm, supportive relationships, access to mental health care, or good physical health are more likely to get disabling depression. People who take better care of their physical health, take time to relax and do things they enjoy, and spend meaningful time with people they love each day are less likely to have depression.

It's easy to ignore our feelings or troubling thoughts. However, it's also dangerous to isolate ourselves. Social support and qualified experts can help us care for any thoughts and feelings that threaten to overwhelm us.

Caring for our mental health isn't just a *nice* thing to have. It's a *must* have.

It's for our sanity. It's for our well-being. It's for our peace of mind.

It's for our family.

The great news about mental health is that we can be vigilant in this area in a very positive way. When we focus on the mentally *healthy* things in our lives – the things that make us feel great – we improve any negative or painful areas by default. Don't believe me? Try it.

An active, growing mind is a healthier mind. Case in point; my church sponsors, the ones who helped our family come from Vietnam, are now ages 90 and 95. Despite having lived longer than most people ever will, they continue to be as sharp as ever. They conduct weekly reading groups and go bowling. My brother and I were blessed to join them a few years ago. What a humbling blast.

Our sponsors accomplished this by being engaged in supportive relationships, community, and service – such as the profound service they performed for my family by making it possible for us to come over from Vietnam.

They have never stopped in their service, enjoyment, and cultivation of positive relationships. Recent research actually shows empirically that this kind of connected, active, warmly social life actually *does* lead to longer lifespan![41]

As any mental health professional will tell you, feeling sad or angry sometimes is okay. In fact, these emotions are a *necessary* part of life, and it is *healthy* to feel them when bad things happen.

But it is *also* necessary to get social support when we feel sad – and the friendly ear of a qualified professional when social support is not sufficient to help you reach your goals.

One important technique used by mental health professionals and pastors alike is this: helping us to re-frame the bad things that happen to us, or around us, as positives.

That may sound crazy or hard to do. But in fact, it is a skill that can be easily learned.

It really is true that when one door closes, another opens. If my childhood had not been as difficult as it was, for example, I would not be as good at my Superpower! I would not have so much power to help organizations function better and serve people all over the world.

So next time you have a misfortune, ask yourself: what doors are open now? What opportunities for growth exist now that did not exist before?

It's okay to feel down in the dumps sometimes. You know what? It's normal! So long as you notice when your feelings start to become too much to manage alone and get the help you need, you will be great.

Vanessa Van Edwards is a bestselling author and behavioral investigator. She makes an interesting observation about how happiness and working our mental health can help us. She's found that, far from being a "selfish" or "unnecessary" pursuit, mental health care and good mental health practices result in:

Increased Income: A University College of London study found that people who are happy as young adults go on to earn more

---

[41] Holt-Lunstad, J., Smith, T., & Layton, J. (2010). Social Relationships and Mortality Risk: A Meta-analytic Review. *SciVee*. doi: 10.4016/19865.01

than their peers later in life.[42] Researchers at Wharton Business School independently found that companies with happy employees outperform the stock market year on year. This may be because we make better decisions and are more creative when we are happy![43]

More Friends: Happy people have more friends and are deemed overall more pleasant, helpful and sociable.[44] This doesn't mean it's bad to feel sad or ask for social support – but when we are helping ourselves by taking real action for our mental health, our good mood becomes contagious!

Higher Productivity: Warwick University Economics professors found that happy people are more productive–a full 12% more - after being put into a good mood.[45]

Live Longer: Happier people live longer, have a lower risk of heart disease and are 50% less likely to get a cold.[46] This may be because stress hormones released by loneliness and depression actually suppress our immune systems and can raise our blood pressure and narrow our arteries.

The source article notes that focusing on becoming happy as an end unto itself can actually *interfere* with becoming happy. But don't worry - that's why the other five sections of our Life Map are

[42] Doward, J., & Graaf, M. de. (2012, March 25). Happy Adolescents "Likely to Have Higher Income" as Adults. Retrieved from https://www.theguardian.com/society/2012/mar/25/happy-people-earn-more-money

[43] Edmans, A., Li, L., & Zhang, C. (2014). Employee Satisfaction, Labor Market Flexibility, and Stock Returns Around The World. doi: 10.3386/w20300

[44] Carter, C. (n.d.). Is Happiness Actually Important? Retrieved from https://greatergood.berkeley.edu/article/item/is_happiness_actually_important

[45] New Study Shows We Work Harder When We Are Happy. (n.d.). Retrieved from https://warwick.ac.uk/newsandevents/pressreleases/new_study_shows/

[46] The Problem with Happiness. (n.d.). Retrieved from https://www.psychologytoday.com/us/blog/curious/201009/the-problem-happiness

dedicated to things that *accidentally* cause happiness when we pursue them.

Happier Friends: Happier people have happier friends–yes, really! Psychologist James H. Fowler studied the data of 5,000 people over 20 years and found that happiness benefits other people through three degrees of connection and that the effects last for a year. He says: "We found a statistical relationship not just between your happiness and your friends' happiness, but between your happiness and your friends' friends' friends' happiness." This may be because happy emotions really are contagious![47]

Better Life: If that all weren't enough, happiness feels freakin' awesome!

> *"Happiness doesn't just flow from success; it actually causes it."*
>
> *-Dr. Richard Wiseman*

Do whatever you need to do to continually grow your mind, discipline it, so that it remains strong, joyful and positive. If what you're doing on your own isn't accomplishing your goals, don't be afraid to reach for professional help.

Your Challenge: Take the same challenge as your physical health concerns, only focus on your mental attitude and how you feel emotionally as markers of success.

Mental Health:

- Where do I want/need to grow mentally?
- What do I want to accomplish in this area in the next year?

---

[47] Oppong, T. (2019, August 21). When You Hang Out With Happy People, You Tend to Feel Happier. Retrieved from https://www.theladders.com/career-advice/when-you-hang-out-with-happy-people-you-tend-to-feel-happier

- Have I been able to accomplish my mental health and life goals on my own so far? If not, might I benefit from seeing if a therapist can help me with these?
- How can I work toward my mental health goal every single day?

Mental Health is about mind training as much as it is about being a lifelong learner.

Where do you want to continually grow? What books do you want to read this year? Where do you want to grow your mind more?

Core Area 3: Daily Financial Focus

Financial chains are some of the most stressful burdens that cause heartache, anxiety and panic for people. Finances can affect our ability to afford shelter, food, and in the U.S., medical and mental health care.

We've discussed in earlier chapters how money makes the world go round. As a universal medium of exchange, it's the best way to ensure we can get anything we might need.

But many people and corporations also succumb to the dark side of money: becoming obsessed with it, hoarding it, prioritizing it over relationships and activities that cause happiness, and even doing unethical or illegal things to obtain it.

All of those reasons make it essential that we find a way to pay the bills ethically and legally – without allowing our financial health to interfere with our mental, physical, relationship, or spiritual health.

Believe it or not, this *is* possible for everyone with strategic planning a round spending, earning, and saving. If done right, we can provide security for ourselves, our family, and others we might be able to positively impact when our finances are in order.

In our society, everyone has *some kind* of financial obligation. Whether we're paying for rent or mortgages, prescriptions or student loans, or countless other expenses – very few people can go through their daily lives without spending money. When making a financial health plan, determining how to pay those *most basic expenses* is step one. When those are taken care of, an immense burden is lifted from our minds.

I desire you to be in a *healthy* financial state, regardless of your obligations. This is a state where we are in control of our finances and we are *not* living paycheck to paycheck or worse, taking on debt we have no clear way to pay back.

What happens to you, your state of mind, and your physical well-being when you are unable to pay your bills? We all know the answer. It's *not* good. In fact, it can become a downward spiral: when we can't afford healthcare or formal education, it can be hard to start earning more.

Whether it takes months or years, I want you to get to a financial state where you no longer feel burdened by not having enough money.

I want you to be in a place where you can develop your skills and help others with your money, because you have more than you need.

I want you to be philanthropic with it. I want you to have enough money to set aside for your kids' futures, for your retirement, for your place of worship and even have some left over after that!

Can you imagine such a state? That is my hope for you!

And believe it or not, it is possible. Just like when running a company, you simply need to be strategic when running your life.

If you already have enough money to meet you and your family's needs, remember this: you can't take your money with you. It's said that "shrouds don't have pockets" because it's well-known that the deceased can't take money or material possessions into the next life. Instead, wealth and material goods can only be used by the living.

If you have enough money to pay your bill and save for retirement, how are you using your extra money to serve others, or future generations of your family?

Financial security is important for our basic physical needs, and our access to things that can help us to thrive and grow. But the worth of a human life isn't measured in dollar amounts. Remember this.

If I were to ask you how much you are worth in dollars, what would be your response? As crazy as this sounds, I'm willing to bet that most of you would pause and actually try to come up with a number!

And yet if I ask you how much your kids are worth in dollars, *none* of you would even hesitate to say that there *is no dollar amount.* They are priceless.

Well you know what? You are priceless too. Stop undervaluing yourself.

Financial security is easier said than done. So is valuing yourself *regardless of your financial situation.* But both can be accomplished with strategic planning and consistent daily action. We'll discuss some tips below.

Your Challenge: Start creating yearly financial goals, if you are not already doing so. Questions to ask yourself might include:

1. What are your household's bare minimum monthly operating expenses?
2. How much ensures that you can have shelter and food, pay off any debts you might have, and have health insurance coverage? This is your monthly minimum earning goal.

    I encourage you to really come up with a *minimum*, not including luxuries and needlessly expensive options. This will give you more "wiggle room" to use your budget to achieve your most important goals.
3. What are you spending *beyond* this minimum budget? Is that really the most rewarding use of that money? Does it give you long-term peace of mind, valuable experiences with the most important people in your life, or useful skills?
4. Do you have an emergency fund? Would you have more peace of mind if you *did* have one?
5. If you are not making enough to meet your basic spending and saving goals, is there a way to change that?
6. Is there a higher-paying job you might be qualified for, or that you might become qualified for easily by taking some classes?

7. If you are having trouble finding a job or switching industries, is there a job search book or a local community center that offers resume or interview training?
8. If you are making more than you need, how much do you want to give every year?
9. How much do you want to invest?
10. Do you have an emergency fund, a vacation budget, and savings goals?
11. What do I need to work on personally, to get to the point where I believe that I am truly a priceless being?
12. How can I work toward my immediate financial goal every single day?

Whole books exist about maximizing your earning potential and your spending, savings, and investment strategies. There are many programs that help you to align your finances with your higher purpose in life. Financial Peace University by Dave Ramsey is an example.

At the end of the day, keeping money and finances in perspective is key. Money doesn't define you or determine your worth by any measure. But when you learn to optimize your management and leveraging of your finances, you are able to do more of what you love in every other area.

Financial Health is about ensuring you have peace of mind when it comes to your finances. Although all sections of the Life Road Map are important, this one is especially important to me and my wife because we grew up extremely poor and had to battle our poor mentality at the same time.

Financial Health is NOT only about financial hoarding, but is ALSO About Financial Stewardship! Money is power, and the question of how we use our power determines our level of fulfillment. Money that is being used to build a future or help others gives us more fulfillment than money that is sitting in the bank or in a fleet of empty vacation homes!

Core Area 4: Daily Family and Relationship Focus

Having a daily family and relationship focus means ensuring we find time to intentionally connect with the important people in our lives. A wise person, Richard Moss, once reminded his students, that: "The greatest gift you can give another is the purity of your attention."

Just listening and remembering the little things about our friends and family can make all the difference in the world.

So how can we effectively practice a daily family and relationship focus? Simply live in the moment with our family and be there for them.

The greatest present we can give is our presence. This means not only being physically present in the room, but even more so being present with our *attention*. We can even do this via text messages during our workday.

Of course, being *mentally* present in our homes on a daily basis can be easier said than done. In fact, *before* I step into my home each day, I have a daily routine that puts my mind and attitude in the right place.

I turn off the car, take a deep breath, and simply say to myself: "Rubi, be present for your family. They have *nothing* to do with the challenges of your work. They are more important than those things. Love them, be there for them, period."

Then I remind myself of what each family member cares about. I can give a listening ear for my wife, a playmate for my son, a hug for my mother-in-law.

Then, and only then, do I go physically enter my home.

Most of us will spend more time at work than at home during our careers. But the *most important thing* is not the *amount* of time we give our families, but the *quality* of attention, presence, and listening we give them.

Your Challenge: Make a list of your important family and friends. Think about what they need *most* from you in terms of your presence.

Then think about who needs your presence *most* today and be present for them. Repeat this each day, and watch your relationships and wellbeing transform.

Family and Relationship Health Questions:

1. What is my role in the most important relationships in my life?
2. Who do I need to be more present for, regardless whether they are near or far away?
3. Who needs to feel more support from me? Encouragement from me?
4. Who supports *me* most? How can I be there for them more?
5. What do I want to accomplish in this area in the next year?
6. How do I best connect with these people on their terms, to show I want them in my life?

Relationship Health is about ensuring the most important people in your life are not forgotten and receive your presence, energy, attention and time. It's also important to consider who nourishes and supports *you* the most. Those are the most valuable relationships to nurture.

Every relationship is different, and so your role in each relationship you have will be unique. Be clear and specific on what you'd like to achieve and accomplish with each individual. Is it more communication, presence, or engagement?

Core Area 5: Daily World Impact (or, Your Area of Service)

You *are* having a world impact regardless of how *big or small* you perceive your role to be. Again, world impact is *not* about size and quantity, but the measure of *quality* of the impact you have on the people whose lives you touch. Doing things for others that bring both them and us joy, peace and happiness.

This can happen in interpersonal relationships, in a volunteer capacity, and even at work. But the important thing is that we are *are* having a positive impact on others, and on the world. This is not just important to some outside party: it is important to our own personal fulfillment and wellbeing.

Focus on the service mentality. Unless we are in a dire, unhealthy work circumstance, there is a way we can serve others by being there. Trust, be present, and serve – and watch how your impact ultimately serves and helps others.

Shoot for the stars and the haughty goals. The first step to accomplishing or creating something great is to imagine it. Dream big in order to serve big.

The most important people around your area of world impact are simply the people right in front of you. You will impact them, whether you set out to do so or not.

Whether you serve a few people or many, you may change lives. Whether you gather one cup of ocean or one drop of ocean or the entire ocean, it is all the same ocean.

If you really get this analogy, you'll stop trying to conquer the entire planet like I once tried in my life. You'll stop running, chasing, feeling like you aren't doing enough.

You'll start believing and realizing the power of the ways you serve every day, even if you feel like you cannot solve the big problems. You will begin to believe you are where you are supposed to be.

I have seen many more individuals happy because they know *who* they are and their purpose. They did valuable work that no one else could. *Not* because they are trying to conquer and climb all the mountain peaks on planet Earth, but because they focused on doing what *they* could do well.

Your Challenge: World Impact is *not* a distant destination, but a daily journey of being more focused on service to others. It means combining our talents, our passions, and our time, and finding a place where there is a legitimate need for our services. This can be big or small, formal or personal. Determine how you can serve others in a healthy way that is mutually beneficial to you and others.

World Influence/Area of Service:

1. How can I leverage my Superpower in this area?
2. Where do I want to leave my mark on this earth?
3. Who am I called to serve?
4. Where am I called to serve?
5. What do I want to be doing most of the time when it comes to work?
6. How would I like to serve?
7. How can I serve in my daily life, in the places I already go?
8. Where do I believe I can be an influence on others?
9. What would I like to accomplish in this area this year?
10. How can I work toward that goal every single day?

Obviously, your career field is one area where you can serve. But you can also serve in your personal relationships or in volunteer capacities unrelated to your career. Just remember to consider how your Superpower can be used to help!

Core Area 6: Daily Spiritual Focus

This title might raise eyebrows for some, because there is a great deal of confusion around the term "spiritual."

What is "spirituality," exactly? Is it religion? Something *other* than religion? Something indefinable?

Spirituality has been practiced by religious and non-religious sages alike for millennia. Modern writers like Eckhart Tolle have created a religion-friendly, yet not religion-dependent, window into incredible peace and bliss that is possible through cultivation of practices.

A non-religious way to understand spirituality is our relationship to something greater than ourselves. Some certainly see this as God and God's creation. Others might think of it as their place in "the big picture" and the ultimate purpose for their existence. There are many theological and philosophical books out there discussing where we came from and why each one of us is here.

However we think about spirituality, research is clear that it *is* beneficial to think about it. People do better when they have a clear sense of purpose and belonging – both in their immediate families, and in "the big picture." Feeling that we know who we are and what we were put here to do, in a cosmic sense, has huge benefits.

In addition, many specific practices created by spiritual teachers over the millennia turn out to have stunning health benefits. Meditation has been shown by the medical community to improve outcomes in everything from mental health to asthma to open heart surgery, and the same yogic practices which were invented for spiritual enlightenment turn out to be among the most powerful practices available for health and fitness, ranging from joint and spine benefits to improved blood sugar control and lower levels of stress hormones.

So let's end this book with a discussion of the area that is, to me, the most important area of our life. Let's discuss our higher purpose, and our highest self.

Daily Spiritual Focus: How Are You Growing Your Highest Self?

This is the biggest component of *my* Life Map because it has helped me so much with all the other areas. I feel that it helps me tap into my eternal self on a daily basis.

As I've said earlier, we take nothing with us when we leave this Earth. And there is *nothing* physical or outside ourselves that we can depend on 100% of the time.

All things, including your closest relationships, *will* let us down in our life at one time or another. This is not because they are bad or lacking – it is simply because everything, including other people, are finite and limited. No one is capable of doing all things.

There *is* one area however, that will never let you down.

And that is the spiritual aspect of your life. That higher, deeper, infinite side of your life. The perfect oneness with God.

LIFE LESSON: Your Spirit is the only thing that is always with you. You are an infinite soul. What are you doing to nourish your higher self and understanding of why you were put here?

When I started intentionally and faithfully focusing on the spiritual component and growth in my life, I discovered that this work put me on a path of self-awareness and ultimately fulfillment.

I now begin and end each and every day, the same way: in prayer, meditation and renewed gratitude for what I have been given. I read empowering passages from scripture and other sources of inspiration.

To reap the same amazing benefits I have discovered, I encourage each and every person to cultivate a few practices:

1. Cultivate a meditation practice. Countless versions of meditation practices exist. Look for one that works with deep breathing, which science shows can actually change brain activity and lower stress hormones.[48] Most Buddhist and Hindu meditation styles use this tool.
2. Begin and end each day with "a reading from scripture." I put that in quotes because it doesn't actually need to be from a religious or "holy" book. People use scripture for inspiration, motivation, meaning, and truth. Any author or poet who communicates inspiring and profound truths to you can convey these benefits.
3. Begin and end each day with a gratitude practice. Spending time in gratitude for what we have been given makes us more joyful – and helps us to move confidently toward our goals.

---

[48] Relaxation techniques: Try these steps to reduce stress. (2017, April 19). Retrieved from https://www.mayoclinic.org/healthy-lifestyle/stress-management/in-depth/relaxation-technique/art-20045368

Your Challenge: Find inspirational thoughts and routines that are meaningful to you and make them a part of your daily morning routine. Start the day filled with gratitude and you'll be more joyful and peaceful throughout the day.

Do *anything and everything* you need to do to remind yourself each and every day that you are "a spiritual being having a human experience."

Spiritual Health:

1. What inspires me and connects me to my highest, infinite self?
2. How can I truly become *one* with God and infinite source?
3. Where do I want/need to grow spiritually?
4. What do I want to accomplish in this area in the next year?
5. What can I do each day to celebrate my spirituality?

Individuals with spiritual health are more at peace and happy with themselves and toward others.

As with all the areas, it's personally your call as to how much or little you'd like to add here. But I do encourage you to give it a second look – even if you don't normally think of yourself as a spiritual person.

Sources ranging from scientific studies to modern authors have shown that spirituality doesn't have to mean conforming to an existing religion or theological dogma. It can be something we experience for ourselves, and which holds profound benefits.

Now It's Time To Make Your Map!

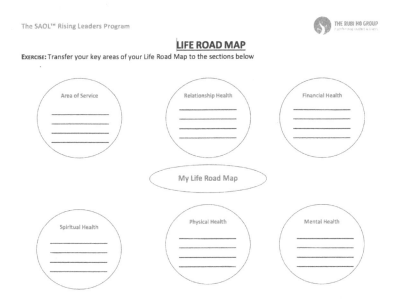

Created by Rubi Ho

Creating Your Affirmation Statement

There is always that seed of doubt that exists within all of us. That doubt seed that says: *"You aren't worthy, you aren't good enough, you don't deserve it!"* Don't believe it!

YOU ARE WORTH IT.

YOU ARE GOOD ENOUGH.

YOU DO DESERVE IT.

I've been doing this exercise now for over a decade. My Life Map has been nothing short of a miracle for me. It will create the same results for you if you give it a try. And to help us along the way, I create something I call my "Ultimate Affirmation Statement." This is a statement of everything we have learned here about our own value and place in this universe.

The affirmation statement is a statement of belief and commitment that all things described in your Life Road Map shall come to pass.

It is a statement that you write not only to yourself, but also to the higher power within yourself. Your highest self. The essence of God in you.

The affirmation is a statement of faith and of belief that propels you toward your goals.

Be vigilant in your life, not passive. Pour all your energy into it. Get every area of your Life Map *healthy*. Create firm, tangible goals behind every item, evaluate your progress at least quarterly, and don't stop until you get there. See if your life doesn't start to change for the better year after year.

Now let's make a statement of affirmation of you, together.

MY ULTIMATE STATEMENT OF AFFIRMATION

I'd like to leave you with my personal statement of affirmation. I have been repeating this affirmation, every single day now, for more than a decade. I was compelled to write down the following words after I came to from a deep state of meditation. I have these words framed in my office and have shared them with countless others. I know them to be true, for me, for you, for the world.

Again, I'm not here to impose any sort of religion or belief on you. When you look at this, you will easily see ways in which a similar statement could be created by a Buddhist, a Muslim, a secular humanist, or any other theological or philosophical persuasion.

Just make sure that you include *your* highest power in your affirmation, to remind you of why you are here.

May you know, as I do, that we are *all* born to be great, and come from greatness.

My Ultimate Affirmation

I am complete as God, Jesus, and Holy Spirit are in me and complete me
I am infinite as my Creator is in me and infinite
I am blessed in abundance financially, in health, family, career and wisdom
I have God's grace and power in me to accomplish any and all things
Being one with God, nothing is impossible and I am never alone
I am showered in abundance in all walks of my life
I am patient, loving, objective, hold no resentment, speak and live out truth
I am wise and filled with the love of I am
I am always seizing the moment and in the moment
Nothing can separate me from the love and power of God in my life
I accomplish and exceed in the realm of abundance and
success whatever I put my mind, heart and soul into
I am protected from temptation and brush off those who
try to tempt me or create resentment in me
I am a light on the mountain
I was created to create, to serve and to love
Amen

Created by Rubi Ho

Here's to creating and living your 'Thrival' Life!

-Rubi

Resources & References

1. Associated Press. Over 30 million U.S. workers will lose their jobs because of AI. MarketWatch. https://www.marketwatch.com/story/ai-is-set-to-replace-36-million-us-workers-2019-01-24. Published January 24, 2019. Accessed February 1, 2020.
2. Amazon mission statement. Retrieved from https://mission-statement.com/amazon/
3. By Payments. (2019, June 14). Retrieved from https://www.pymnts.com/amazon/2019/amazon-share-ecommerce/
4. IBM Archives. Retrieved from https://www.ibm.com/ibm/history/history/history_intro.html
5. Editors of the Encyclopaedia Britannica. Berkshire Hathaway American Company. Retrieved https://www.britannica.com/topic/Berkshire-Hathaway
6. Shell Company History. Retrieved from https://www.shell.com/about-us/our-heritage/our-company-history.html
7. Nintendo History. Retrieved from https://www.nintendo.co.uk/Corporate/Nintendo-History/Nintendo-History-625945.html#1889
8. American Express History. Retrieved from https://about.americanexpress.com/our-history
9. Toys 'R' Us Mission and Vision. Retrieved from http://www.makingafortune.biz/list-of-companies-t/toys-r-us.html
10. Colvin, G. (2018, May 24). GE Decline, What The Hell Happened. Retrieved from https://fortune.com/longform/ge-decline-what-the-hell-happened/

11. Kaplan RS, Norton DP. *The Balanced Scorecard: Translating Strategy Into Action*. Boston, MA: Harvard Business School Press

12. Paolantonio S. *How Football Explains America*. Chicago, IL: Triumph Books; 2015.

13. Madrigal, A. (2019, Feb 7). When Amazon Went From Big to Unbelievably Big. Retrieved from https://www.theatlantic. com/technology/archive/2019/02/when-amazon-went-from-big-to-unbelievably-big/582097/

14. Mui, Ch. (2012, Jan 19) How Kodak Failed. Retrieved from https://www.forbes.com/sites/chunkamui/2012/01/18/how-ko dak-failed/#1540a32c6f27

15. Google Search. Strategy. Retrieved from https://www.google. com/search/strategy

16. Harnish V. *Scaling Up*. How few companies make it and why the rest don't. Ashburn, VA: Gazelles Inc; 2014.

17. Chappelow,J.Porter's5Forces.Retrievedfromhttps://www.inve stopedia.com/terms/p/porter.asp

18. OGSM. (n.d.). Retrieved from https://archpointgroup.com/ voice-of-the-leader-how-ogsm-has-helped-my-company/

19. Cuddy AJC, Glick P, Beninger A. The dynamics of warmth and competence judgments, and their outcomes in organiza tions. *Research in Organizational Behavior*. 2011;31:73-98. doi:10.1016/j.riob.2011.10.004.

20. Schwantes, M. (2017, September 21). Why Do Employees Really Quit Their Jobs? Research Says It Comes Down to These Top 8 Reasons. Retrieved from https://www.inc.com/ why-do-employees-really-quit-their-jobs-research-says-it-comes-down-to-these-top-8-reasons.html

21. Yakowicz, W. (2015, August 21). The True Cost of a Toxic Work Environment. Retrieved from https://www.inc.com/ will-yakowicz/the-cost-of-toxic-environment.html?cid= search

22. Pearson, C. P. C. (2019, March 19). The Price of Incivility, Harvard Business Review. Retrieved from https://hbr.org/2013/01/the-price-of-incivility

23. Rigoni, B., & Nelson, B. (2019, December 16). Few Millennials Are Engaged at Work. Retrieved from https://news.gallup.com/businessjournal/195209/few-millennials-engaged-work.aspx

24. Maxwell, J. The Five Level of Leadership. Retrieved from https://www.skillsoft.com/resources/john-maxwell-the-5-levels-of-leadership/

25. Watkins, D. C. M. D. (2014, August 1). The Successor's Dilemma. Retrieved from https://hbr.org/1999/11/the-successors-dilemma

26. Maquinana, R. (2014, February 9). Mike Tomlin fined $100,000 for actions in Steelers' loss. Retrieved from http://www.nfl.com/news/story/0ap2000000292517/article/mike-tomlin-fined-100000-for-actions-in-steelers-loss

27. Shook, N. (2018, October 10). NFL fines Mike Tomlin $25K for criticism of officials. Retrieved from http://www.nfl.com/news/story/0ap3000000972507/article/nfl-fines-mike-tomlin-25k-for-criticism-of-officials

28. Maxwell, J. C. (2013). *The 5 Levels of Leadership: Proven Steps to Maximise Your Potential*. New York: Center Street.

29. Mcleod, S. (2018, May 21). Maslow's Hierarchy of Needs. Retrieved from https://www.simplypsychology.org/maslow.html

30. Holt-Lunstad, J., Smith, T., & Layton, J. (2010). Social Relationships and Mortality Risk: A Meta-analytic Review. *Sci Vee*. doi: 10.4016/19865.01

31. More Than Job Satisfaction. (n.d.). Retrieved from https://www.apa.org/monitor/2013/12/job-satisfaction

32. The Thing We Fear More Than Death. (n.d.). Retrieved from https://www.psychologytoday.com/us/blog/the-real-story-risk/201211/the-thing-we-fear-more-death

33. Pozin, I. (2016, March 4). The Secret to Happiness? Spend Money on Experiences, Not Things. Retrieved from https://

www.forbes.com/sites/ilyapozin/2016/03/03/the-secret-to-happiness-spend-money-on-experiences-not-things/

34. This Is The New Price Of Happiness - Forbes. (n.d.). Retrieved from https://www.forbes.com/sites/learnvest/2018/02/19/this-is-the-new-price-of-happiness/

35. Dyer, W. W. (2016). *10 Secrets for Success and Inner Peace.* Carlsbad, CA: Hay House, Inc.

36. Why Time Goes Faster as You Get Older. (n.d.). Retrieved from https://www.psychologytoday.com/us/blog/cutting-edge-lead ership/201004/why-time-goes-faster-you-get-older

37. How Health Affects a Child's School Performance. (n.d.). Retrieved from https://health.ucsd.edu/news/2006/Pages/04 07_Taras.aspx

38. Deutschman, A. (2008). *Change or Die: the Three Keys to Change at Work and in Life.* New York: Collins.

39. Renard, G. R. (2010). *The Disappearance of the Universe.* Syndey N.S.W.: RHYW.

40. Depression. (n.d.). Retrieved from https://www.who.int/ news-room/fact-sheets/detail/depression

41. Holt-Lunstad, J., Smith, T., & Layton, J. (2010). Social Rela tionships and Mortality Risk: A Meta-analytic Review. *Sci Vee.* doi: 10.4016/19865.01

42. Doward, J., & Graaf, M. de. (2012, March 25). Happy Adoles cents "Likely to Have Higher Income" as Adults. Retrieved from https://www.theguardian.com/society/2012/mar/25/hap py-people-earn-more-money

43. Edmans, A., Li, L., & Zhang, C. (2014). Employee Satisfac tion, Labor Market Flexibility, and Stock Returns Around The World. doi: 10.3386/w20300

44. Carter, C. (n.d.). Is Happiness Actually Important? Retrieved from https://greatergood.berkeley.edu/article/item/is_happi ness_actually_important

45. New Study Shows We Work Harder When We Are Happy. (n.d.). Retrieved from https://warwick.ac.uk/newsandevents/ pressreleases/new_study_shows/

46. The Problem with Happiness. (n.d.). Retrieved from https://www.psychologytoday.com/us/blog/curious/201009/the-problem-happiness

47. Oppong, T. (2019, August 21). When You Hang Out With Happy People, You Tend to Feel Happier. Retrieved from https://www.theladders.com/career-advice/when-you-hang-out-with-happy-people-you-tend-to-feel-happier

48. Relaxation techniques: Try these steps to reduce stress. (2017, April 19). Retrieved from https://www.mayoclinic.org/healthy-lifestyle/stress-management/in-depth/relaxation-technique/art-20045368

About The Author

Rubi Ho partners with companies as their Organizational Leadership Consultant and Enterprise Executive Coach. His purpose is simply to help people thrive in life, period.

Personally, he has a passion for golf, the relentless pursuit of service to others and spending time with family and friends.

Contact Rubi personally at rubi@therubihogroup.com if you ever desire to:

- Have Rubi Ho be your Keynote Speaker
- Learn more about how to become an Organizational Leadership Consultant and Enterprise Executive Coach yourself!
- Work with him and/or his affiliates at The Rubi Ho Group
- Simply connect with him.

Advanced Praises

"Rubi weaves his compelling life story into his mastery of leadership and what it takes to thrive in work and life! This book is for *anyone* who wants to win! Read, read again and share!"
Kathy Gingrich Lubbers, CEO LEI Executive Coaching and Consulting

"Rubi Ho successfully analyzes the complex dynamics of a fulfilling and effective work/life balance and provides concrete suggestions for its implementation and how to thrive!"
Lou Terhar, Senator, Ohio Senate (Retired) and Former CEO, Indian Motorcycle

"Rubi provides incredible insight and principles that will inspire and transform current and emerging leaders. If you want to be better version of yourself, personally and professionally, this is the book for you."
Duana Patton, CEO-Area Agency on Aging-District 5

"Rubi Ho's "Thrival Guide" is inspirational and motivational. It is a straight forward approach to managing the realities of work and life; one that is sure to guide you through the 'ups and downs', landing you on top of your challenges!"
Dr. Dianne M. Dawson Daniels, Professor of Leadership Studies

"A practical and personal MUST HAVE field manual for work and life that is easy to read and packed with helpful tips in many areas of leadership and self-development. I have watched Rubi demonstrate

his mastery in these areas, and his passion for helping others shines through!"
Kevin Sherd, Sr. Director, National Energy Company

"Rubi lays out a path for optimizing your core competencies and superpowers for a more fulfilled home and work life. I recommend Rubi Ho's Thrival Guide to EVERYONE!"-
Larke U. Recchie, CEO-Ohio Association of Area Agencies on Aging

"Learn how to become the CEO of your own life and be inspired by Rubi Ho! He has personally helped me communicate and think like a CEO and will help you shoot for the stars as well and maybe even dream about colonizing Pluto!"
Kevin Caringer, Executive Director, National Energy Company

"Painful Past, Grounded Reality, Committed Mentoring: Rubi pulls back the terribly painful curtain of his beginnings, devises a series of CORE Life Values and solid Work principals and then mentors you 'home.' Wow! This work is WAY more than a self-help book! It very acutely says, you are not alone, and you have never been alone..............just ask for help, and if no one is there to assist, here is a plan that worked for me.
-I love you brother, and I will never forget what you have done for me.
GT, Chief Revenue Officer